When the Crying's Done

When the Crying's Done

A Journey Through Widowhood

Jeannette Kupfermann

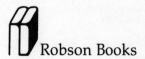

Robson Books

Acknowledgements

I would like to thank all the friends, relatives and colleagues who gave me practical and emotional support during this very difficult time in my life. These include especially my children, Elias and Mina, who both made very useful suggestions for the book and helped with the typing of the first draft; Caroline Fuji, who managed to master my word processor; and editors Louise Dixon and Hilary Engel, whose helpful criticism enabled me to turn my jumbled thoughts into a book.

My thanks, too, to Frankie McGowan, who, as editor of *She* magazine, first encouraged me to write about bereavement, and to Corinna Honan, Rod Gilchrist, Nicholas Gordon, Peter Wright and Linda Kelsey, whose professional support gave me the confidence to take up my writing again.

Finally, my grateful thanks to all those friends and neighbours who provided a lifeline and were simply 'there' for me.

First published in Great Britain in 1992 by
Robson Books Ltd, Bolsover House,
5-6 Clipstone Street, London W1P 7EB

British Library Cataloguing in Publication Data
A catalogue record for this book is available from the British Library

Printed in Great Britain by St. Edmundsbury Press, Bury St. Edmunds, Suffolk

Typeset by EMS Photosetters, Thorpe Bay, Essex

*I dedicate this book
to the loving
memory of
Jacques*

Prologue

In the midst of winter, I finally learned
that there was in me
an invincible summer.

Albert Camus

This book developed from a magazine article I wrote describing my early experiences of widowhood. They called it 'Out of the Shadows'. It received such an overwhelming response, not only from widows, but from people who had experienced other kinds of loss, ranging from illness to divorce, that I realized there was a great need for a book to be written in the first person describing feelings that still, to some extent, remain hidden in our society which is only just breaking its taboo on death. At the time I wrote with a rawness which has only gradually faded – and it was this very rawness that people responded to. Even now, less than four years later, it still surprises, even shocks me, and I am glad I made a record, however incomplete, of these feelings when I did – for, as with the pain of labour, the mind very soon seems to eradicate them.

Death is certain: we all live with that knowledge, and yet somehow there is no way to prepare for it. Nor would we perhaps want to if we could for there can be no dress rehearsal for a look into the abyss. According to statistics many, if not most, married women will one day be left widows, and yet none of us is prepared for widowhood. We have a nebulous vision of living out our lives with our partner. Death cuts this vision short: there will be no growing old together. Suddenly the future does not exist; there is only a looking back.

When I wrote the article I was still very close to my husband Jacques' death. I could scarcely see my way forward – even in terms of a single day. Now, almost four years on, although my grieving has not entirely stopped I am at last starting to feel optimistic for the future again. At the time I felt engulfed in a nightmare from which I would never wake up. I had suffered not one, but two grievous losses: my father died just a few months before Jacques, from a sudden heart attack in my own home. The two men in my life had gone almost simultaneously. I was left with no safety net, no point of anchorage and, above all, caught up in the fast-moving events of my husband's terminal illness and battle for life, no time to digest the first tragedy and work through it since the second was so soon upon me: for I had scarcely begun to mourn my father when I was told that my husband had months, maybe only weeks to live. Suddenly my life seemed to have become a tragedy of almost Greek proportions. I was living in a state of total fear, half expecting another death. Who will be next? I wondered; for death stirs very deep and primitive superstitions within us. I thought of myself as cursed – doomed even. Somewhere in the darker recesses of my mind was the notion that I myself was responsible for all the bad luck: that I had somehow *caused* the deaths, and was being punished. The notion of divine retribution runs very deep. These feelings, I now know, are common for survivors of any tragedy.

In the early days of my widowhood I felt so swamped, so numbed, so battered by events, that my very first feelings were that I would never recover; that I too would be struck down. At the back of my mind was the thought that I would somehow be relieved of my own responsibility for living. I now see this not as a death wish but rather as a sort of self-administered anaesthetic which enabled me to do precisely nothing. It soon became apparent, however, that not only would I go on living but that I would have to take responsibility for others too – for my mother and my children in particular and also for my work and my home, among other things.

I remember my bereavement counsellor saying to me, 'Sometimes all we can do is crawl around at the bottom'. I was grateful to her for these words since that was precisely how it felt. For what seemed like an age to me, I crawled around making no discernable progress whatsoever. Putting the kettle on was a Herculean task. I remember asking Rabbi Hugo Grynn – a survivor of the Auschwitz concentration camp – 'Where can I go to get motivation?' His answer was unequivocal: 'Your motivation will be having to earn a living and look after your family.' And he added: 'Remember your religion says you must mourn for one year, but after that you are expected to join the living. No one will treat you as a mourner.' The blueprint for recovery was there: I had even been given a deadline. Weep and wail for one year – but then, the crying's done. The crying of course, is never altogether done. My journey to recovery is not yet over: it did not happen magically in one year – or even two – but the rabbi's words helped prepare me psychologically.

I have since read many books on grief and bereavement. I have tried to glean something from each of them. I disliked the ones that spoke only about 'stages' of mourning – as if it was some sort of examination one had to pass. I preferred those that showed the positive side of grieving – that at least gave it some meaning. Among those was *Living with Grief* by Dr Tony Lake who writes: 'People who grieve have been forced by events to look rather more deeply at their lives and to re-examine their life purposes and their relationships.' The proposition that grief can be a strengthening experience makes a great deal of sense. The death of somebody close always brings new choices into our lives. I am grateful to Dr Lake for pointing out that grief is not a simple matter of being unhappy: indeed one can have feelings of the greatest happiness even in the throes of the greatest sorrow. Grief is something you *do* – not something that happens to you – an active process, or pathway for you to follow, a journey for which you are responsible. On that journey one is faced with certain tasks which have to do with acceptance, with coming to terms with issues that you may have avoided all your life. On this journey you are forced by events to look more deeply at your life, your aims and all your relationships.

There are many women and men taking this journey. Most do it consciously and make progress. Others falter and never move on: some even travel backwards and a few, tragically, do not survive at all, succumbing to fatal illness or even suicide in the year following the loss of their partner. In fact, I'm not sure that one can rightly describe it as a journey: sometimes it seems more like a roller-coaster ride. There will be a fairly serene period followed by more bleakness: a period of optimism, growth and adjustment followed by leaden inertia. I wish I could say it was smoother, neater, less chaotic – but everyone I have spoken to suffering similar loss agrees that it isn't.

This book – which draws on the journals I have kept over the years – is dedicated to my many fellow travellers: to all those picking up the pieces of a shattered world, slowly re-assembling their lives: to all those who feel locked in endless greyness – to tell them that there is 'an invincible summer' in us all, and in the hope that my account will give them some encouragement and hope.

Chapter One

The Long Hard Winter

'Black is night's cope,
But death will not appal
One who, past doubtings all,
Waits in unhope.'

Thomas Hardy, *In Tenebris*

My long hard winter started in October 1987. I walked through the door of the hospital with a sense of foreboding. Jacques had been sent there, after months of uncertainty and increasing pain and sickness, for a body scan. When I saw what looked to me like ghosts flitting past – patients with heads bald from radio-therapy, in their white gowns – I somehow sensed I was looking death in the face, and I was filled with dread as my severely wasted husband was delivered into a huge washing machine-like contraption. It was as if he were going on a journey to the 'other side' – and perhaps nothing could be more hellish than the battle the terminal cancer victim has to fight. I knew I would fight it with him till the end.

Our partnership had endured twenty-three years. I had met Jacques through a blind date in New York in 1964 when I was feeling at a low ebb, having just been jilted by the young medical student who was my real reason for crossing the Atlantic, although I pretended to be working on a Masters degree. At the same time, as well as studying at Columbia University, I was working as research librarian at the Wenner-Gren Foundation for Anthropological Research – and sharing a flat on East 82nd Street with another anthropologist. One day I received a call from a friend: 'There's this great guy who'd like to meet you. He's an artist in his late thirties – very charming and you'll like him. I've given him your number.' My heart sank: I'd never been on a blind date in my life. When he called I decided to do the very British thing of inviting him to tea: that way, if I didn't like him I could get rid of him by the evening. Five minutes before he was due to arrive he called again to ask if he could bring his dog, Sam. This was a new one on me: men didn't usually bring their pets on a first date. But since I loved animals, I readily agreed. Sam turned out to be a cartoonist's dream: a cross between a basset hound and a beagle – and so attached was Jacques to this endearing creature that when travelling around Europe he had built a special carrier for him on the back of his motorbike. Jacques, in a huge leather World War One airman's coat, was dark and craggy, and bore a striking resemblance to Humphrey Bogart. I was immediately struck by his air of quiet intensity and knew that I definitely didn't want to get rid of him before dark! Instead I jumped at his invitation to dinner that evening in the Village. He then offered to drive me anywhere I wanted in his battered VW bus.

It was January, and heavy snow in New York City made it seem almost like fairyland, especially in Central Park with the contrast between the huge white areas and the skyscrapers with twinkling lights. This part of the city at night had always enchanted me. Childishly, I asked Jacques if he would drive me round Central Park six times: he said yes. The next day he proposed on a deserted beach in New Jersey: this time, *I* said yes. We weren't actually married until five months later in England – and, it must be said, not without some trepidation on my part. Not only was Jacques seventeen years older than I was but, while we were both Jewish, our backgrounds were very different. I had been born in Surrey, England, he in Vienna. His background was the Holocaust, and although he escaped from Austria in 1939 on one of the special children's trains (Kinder Transporte) – going first to Holland and then to the United States where he had family – his parents did not manage to escape, and were eventually deported by the Nazis and murdered.

The early years of our marriage were spent in America. We moved from a fifth-floor 'walk up' on Riverside Drive, New York City to Woodstock in upstate New York when I was pregnant with our son Elias in the first year of our marriage. Although we only lived there for two years Woodstock represented the beginning of our relationship together: it was the place of all our early hopes, where like any newly-weds we found our first house – a little colonial farmhouse on Ohayo Mountain where we had Bob Dylan as our neighbour and a brook running through two acres of wild garden.

The Woodstock years were good ones: we arrived two years in advance of the famous pop festival and were still there when it happened. We were always entertaining – these were the party years: 'hat parties', exotic parties, twenties parties, barbecues – even, it was rumoured, 'orgies'. There was the excitement of local girl Pam Feeley marrying her childhood sweetheart Lee Marvin. That was Woodstock in the sixties; a place where fortunes changed as fast as marriage partners. In many ways, it seemed to be a crucible for the rest of America – that is, artistic and musical America, for it had money, talent, useful proximity to

New York and the space and tranquillity of wood and mountains.

It also had a serious drug problem (albeit 'soft drugs' – the 'crack' epidemic had not yet struck), which was one of the reasons why, in 1970, we decided to leave Woodstock and make our home in England. The other reason was that we wanted our children to grow up surrounded by family – aunts, uncles, grandparents – and as Jacques had virtually no relatives, we could only achieve this by returning to England where I was one of four children and part of a large family. Marrying Jacques, a Holocaust victim, I was very aware that he wanted to replace the family he had lost, though this at times was to conflict with his drive for artistic independence and freedom.

And indeed the first couple of years back in London proved especially traumatic: we now had a second child – our daughter Mina – Jacques had few contacts, and we were housed in a damp flat in North London. Our move to England had left us broke. I found work as a model with the Cherry Marshall Agency – which didn't prove very easy with two babies under the age of three. I had lost a lot of weight, without even being aware of it, and seemed to have a perpetual cough, diagnosed as 'bronchitis' by a series of doctors. One night I was taken violently ill with a temperature of 106 degrees. It was pneumonia; but the Irish locum who had been called out in the emergency took one look and realized that I had something even worse, something he had seen many times in poverty-stricken areas of Ireland: TB.

It is ironic that at that time I was the fragile one and Jacques had to worry about me, for the drugs they gave me to cure the tuberculosis played havoc with my immune system and for several years I succumbed to every illness going.

Meanwhile I had a toddler and a baby to look after – and I thanked God they had been unaffected by my illness (TB is not strictly speaking contagious). I tried to do all the normal things a mother did in this period: and having Jacques at home meant he could take over the parenting when I was unable to do it. We had so little money that Jacques was forced to take a menial job and I, unable to model, found some work translating an anthropology book from French to English which I could do at home.

The doctor had recommended that as soon as I was sufficiently cured we should move out of London. Jacques wanted a bigger home with a studio too. Gradually, my strength returned – though it took me almost ten years to get my immune system back to normal. A stroke of luck came my way when someone recommended me (because of some earlier articles I had written) as an advisor on Hassidic history to film director Fred Zinnemann, who was thinking of making a film of the classical folk tale *The Dybbuk* (The Devil). Fred was willing to employ me as technical advisor in his Mount Street offices in Mayfair, which meant that I could afford some part-time help with the children and that Jacques could give up the odd jobs and get on with his painting. We had also had an offer on our Woodstock house. Now was the time to start thinking of moving out of London.

I had seen a rambling Regency house in Berkshire advertised in *The Sunday Times*. It seemed an incredible bargain. We saw it on a cold, grey February day and even then I remember being struck by the charm of the ironwork balconies entwined with trailing forsythia. It reminded me of New Orleans where we had both spent a lot of time. It was fairly dilapidated, crammed full of antiques and junk – but I fell in love instantly with its light spacious rooms with lofty ceilings and marble fireplaces. As I walked up the garden path and looked at the orchard with its apple and pear trees I had such a strong sense of *déjà vu* that I knew we had to make an offer there and then. It was the house I had always fantasized about, although it was in a far from dream state and would need a year of work – not to mention cleaning. We never had the money to decorate the house quite as we wished but somehow over the years we managed to do little bits and pieces – and despite the never-ending saga of blocked drains, over-flowing gutters, brick walls that needed pointing, draughty rooms and leaks, the whole effect, if you didn't look too closely, was charming. I never grew out of love with it, and although at times I cursed it for the demands it made upon us, and for its sheer lack of comfort, emotionally and physically it was our island. Over the period of Jacques' illness and my subsequent years of bereavement it was – and it remains – a great comfort.

Two years later, after a particularly successful show (Jacques had by now managed to find a London gallery to exhibit his work), we bought Fuchsia Cottage on the coast in north Cornwall – an impulse buy after we had spent several very happy holidays in that area. We had discovered the little fishing village one grey November. We had been driving around in the rain for hours trying to find a friendly cafe or hotel that was open out of season, without much success, when a local pointed us in the direction of the nearest signs of life. As we came over the top of a hill it emerged out of the mist and rain like some enchanted

'Brigadoon', with its twinkling lights, winding High Street, smuggler's inns and pastel houses built into the cliffs. We couldn't believe our eyes, it looked so magical. Best of all there was a welcoming hotel. Jacques fell instantly in love with the stark beauty of the Atlantic views which particularly appealed to him. He had always been a 'winter man', preferring the greys and blacks of Northern scenery to anything exotic and sunny.

We found the cottage just as instantly 'magical'. I was lying on a beach at Daymer Bay – that lovely curve of white sand and dunes overlooked by a green hill – and Jacques was driving around looking for a local paper, as we had vaguely entertained the idea of buying a small property in the area. He came back very excited saying he had just seen a cottage in the village itself – but that we would have to decide there and then whether we wanted it. There was no question of a surveyor or biding our time. It had to be instant. I threw a shirt on over my bikini and rushed down to see it.

The cottage itself was very basic and homely, with low-beamed ceilings and white plaster-board walls, and contained just a few sticks of old furniture. The front courtyard had chipped uneven paving stones and a crumbly old shed obscuring the light. But there too were its glories: fuchsia bushes – or more accurately, trees – that grew almost as high as the three-storey Victorian house. And the situation was enchanting: it lay just one street back from the harbour in one of the narrowest alleyways I had ever seen – known locally as 'Squeezy Belly Alley' – which had other higgledy-piggledy white-washed cottages leaning over each other with little corners bright with flowers spilling out of baskets and tubs. The interior was far from glamorous: it had been a 'holiday let' for years.

Yet shabby though the cottage was I knew that it was for us. In the early days, before I worked anything like full-time, I would take the children down there for six to eight weeks at a time. Even when it rained (and it did often) we would amuse ourselves playing hours of Monopoly or painting pebbles. I remember organizing snail races on the wet sands in the harbour to keep the children amused, and getting them to devise 'snail gardens'. We were joined by other friends, with their children, who rented cottages round about, and we would take it in turns to cook vast mackerel suppers for the hungry hordes. The children formed a little colony, which left the adults free to read or sunbathe on the glorious beaches. They would run in and out of each other's cottages, and spending summers together gave their lives some measure of continuity. Twice a week they would drag us down to the Platt to listen to the Bodmin Brass Band. We would all gather round and gaze at the hills in the distance as the band oom-pah-pahed away – later to follow them Pied Piper style up the hill and down again in a traditional 'floral dance'.

I particularly associated the cottage with Jacques, who would spend time there alone in the winter, sometimes going on fishing trips with Elias, or simply setting off for the clifftops canvas, easel and paints on his back, struggling with the elements to secure them in some wild and windy spot. I associate it too with the many friends we had there in common: entertaining them to saffron cake and tea on our little patio, which we smartened up a little by knocking down the dilapidated shed and re-paving. Together we planted a small tree in a pot to provide shade, and together too we would cut back the luxuriant fuchsia. Jacques, as with everything else in our garden, loved it overgrown, wild and tangled, and the cutting-back was only done to appease neighbours who complained it overhung into the narrow alleyway. Fuchsia Cottage, like the house, was to become a sanctuary for me after Jacques died, though at first the sheer responsibility of maintaining it filled me with desolation. It took a while before I felt comfortable walking up the overgrown path.

Perhaps the most painful and difficult part of writing this book has been remembering and describing Jacques' cruel illness itself. It was something I blocked out for a long time, until a newspaper headline proclaiming that Rex Harrison had died of cancer of the pancreas jolted me into remembering and looking back at the detailed journal I kept at the time. I go back and relive the grief of that winter of 1987.

> Jacques reclines in the 'relaxing' garden chair – his swollen legs on Mina's needlework stool – pillows in his back. His face is pale, shrunken, hollow-eyed, with a look of desperation – his lips colourless: with his wispy white hair he looks so heart-breakingly frail, the little orphaned boy, and my heart is heavy with anguish for him.
>
> I feel every pain – every twinge in his achingly sore diaphragm. The illness has raged now for three or so months – first the diarrhoea – then the terrible pain – then the

swellings on his ankles, legs and lumps on his shoulders, arms and hands. His whole body is like one open wound – and I weep. I weep for this man I love above everything and everyone else: who has been my mother, father, friend, lover, comforter and mentor – my constant companion and ally – my husband of twenty-three years.

I pray silently for him – and all the time I fear the emptiness, the nothingness to come. I try not to grieve in advance. I sit with him at the hospital as he waits for his CT scan – and see him emerge shocked and traumatized. I watch the ghost-like patients in their dressing gowns: the husbands comforting wives, daughters and mothers – and again, I weep for all of them . . .

That night he goes into shock: he is deeply depressed and does not want to stay in the house. We walk for an hour or so in the chill damp night air, my arm around his shrunken body. I feel closer than I have ever felt to him. I pick him a white rose from a garden on the hill and I have a vision of a white lily with a light shining on it. Tomorrow he will get the results. Jacques says he feels a sudden fear that he will not last the night. I give him whisky and water, and read him Psalm 112. He sleeps in his special chair by the side of my bed – and wakes, as usual, several times in the night.

We survive the night together. Another day dawns – and again, I start the breakfast – shop for calves' liver, make soup and wait. I think of our walks in Cliveden, the Japanese water garden he loves so . . . and I love him too – this poor frail pain-ridden man, clutching at my hand beside me in the bed, propped up on pillows, the man who has been by my side for all these years – my *everything*. I want to take his pain into me. I pray, I read Psalms – I prepare the special vegetable and fruit juices he has been prescribed as part of the anti-cancer diet – do the lengthy washing out of the juice extractor machine – worry about him as he takes shaky walks on the terrace, listen for him as he spends long sessions in the bathroom with his radio. I watch his grey face over breakfast – anxiously listen to his breathing at night – listen to him heaving and writhing in pain – my man – the being I love most in the world who has given such love, beauty and devotion so silently, so undemandingly all these years, and my anguish knows no bounds. I want to tear out my hair – weep and wail – and yet I restrain myself – keep calm – keep coping – keep reassuring – present a face of optimism – go through the visualization exercises with him – relax him – stroke his hand, face and white hair – and devise a battle song to defeat this wicked disease.

'In the spring,' he sings, 'I will be better . . .'

When the doctor told me that Jacques had only a very short time to live and left it to me to tell him, Jacques at first greeted the news with disbelief. Then he quickly decided that if there was any chance of a cure anywhere whatsoever in the world he would try it. In desperation I phoned friends in France, America and Israel to learn if there was anything – anything at all that might give us some hope. He was, it seemed, too 'advanced' to be put on an Inteferon/Interleukon programme a friend was running, but someone in New York mentioned a Yugoslav doctor called Stephan Durovic, practising in Geneva, who had pioneered a serum called Krebiozen which had cured two of her friends in quite advanced stages of cancer. We quickly read through the literature, and Jacques decided there and then that there was not a minute to lose. He urged me to call Dr Durovic in Geneva to see if he would take him on as a patient.

Durovic was a man in his eighties and took few patients: nonetheless when I called he told me he would be willing to do the initial blood tests and that if we could come immediately he would book us in at the clinic. Jacques wanted to stay at a first-class hotel, regardless of expense – and I understood this. Above all he sought comfort and service. Within an hour I had booked hotel, flight and arranged a wheelchair at the airport. I knew this had boosted Jacques' morale no end – as he now felt that at least he was doing *something*.

The doctor in England with his 'I'm afraid there is nothing more we can do for you' had severely demoralized Jacques – made him feel 'written off'. I now believe very strongly that whatever the reality no doctor should ever do this – that they should always leave some glimmer of hope. It is so often because orthodox medicine writes them off that the terminally ill turn to alternative healers who at least make them feel more than simply failed machines.

Having made the arrangements to go to Switzerland
I felt a mixture of exhilaration, anticipation, and
tremendous anxiety. Jacques was already so weak that
he required regular blood transfusions to keep him
alive at all. He was also heavily addicted to the
morphine which the doctors had given him almost
immediately, automatically. At the back of my mind
was the thought that I might come back a widow, and I
worried about the possible difficulties of bringing his
body home – though of course I didn't want Jacques to
know what I was thinking. I had to give the impression
of total confidence and calm. It was the hardest task I
had ever performed in my life, and I know that many
wives faced with the knowledge of the terminal nature
of their husband's illness are put in the same position.

Here is a journal extract from Geneva:

'The Ramada *Renaissance*,' repeats Jacques.
'You see, it is significant – renaissance, re-
birth.' He saw something almost mystical in
the name itself, grasping at straws of course.
As we walk into the luxurious but restrained
lobby of the hotel its sense of orderliness
confronts us in our desperation . . . desperation for a *cure*. Dr Durovic, a man of fine
features and sculptured noble head, seated in
the study of his hilltop Cologny home, seems
to sense this. 'I will fight for you,' he says, and
Jacques breathes again.

From our long hotel balcony where Jacques
forces himself to walk up and down every so
often you can see the cockerel on the weather
vane: this fills him with hope, and I hear him
singing to it. The sky is a brilliant blue, the air

crisp as we walk slowly by the harbour and feed the swans. We visit the supermarket and buy grapes, spinach and carrots to feed the juicer which I keep in the bathroom. The same diet that we kept to at home is maintained religiously here, where we revel in the superb room service. I order the calves' liver for Jacques and a bowl of vegetable soup for myself each lunchtime. Jacques arranges and rearranges his pillows on the bed. The swelling is worsening: Jacques can scarcely get his shoes on – but we still go down to walk at night in the streets around the hotel – the Red Light district with scrawny girls in doorways.

The hotel staff greet us with curiosity. Jacques' heavy coat hides the swelling but the face is gaunt and wasted, the eyes hollow under the red beret he wears for both warmth and bravado.

'Monsieur is ill?' one young Portuguese waiter asks at breakfast, where Jacques still helps himself to cereal, fruit and eggs, and enjoys the five-star generosity.

'It's what I always wanted,' he says, 'a first-class hotel. It's like a second honeymoon.' And we sit and watch *Planet of the Apes* on the television in our room, or play eternal Scrabble.

There is a sense of unreality about our being cocooned in this way – but it provides us with an ephemeral feeling of security.

In spite of the good Dr Durovic's encouragement,

and the morale-boosting effect of being in the invigorating, crisp Swiss air in beautiful surroundings, the treatment itself could have very little real effect, as the cancer was already on the liver and too far gone. The daily visits to the clinic and blood tests themselves proved very exhausting for Jacques who, at this point, could only survive on blood transfusions. The withdrawal from morphine exacerbated certain things too: he would swing between drowsiness and hallucination – sometimes, to the alarm of onlookers, in a public place like a restaurant. We kept to a routine of meticulous attention to diet – juicing pounds of carrots, grapes and green vegetables, eating mainly in the hotel room – while at the same time taking a twice-daily walk by the lake, sometimes stopping off at a little patisserie for a hot chocolate and pastry. Jacques would walk slowly with difficulty and leaning on my arm – occasionally stopping to feed the swans. In the evening we would dine in the hotel restaurant – afterwards taking another short stroll.

By the end of ten days, Dr Durovic could gauge the results of the blood tests, and if they so indicated, start the treatment. He told us honestly that the X-rays and tests indicated that there was not too much hope Jacques would beat the disease – but that the Krebiozen might prolong his life a little, and lessen the suffering. Jacques was glad to get the truth, and, in spite of becoming increasingly weak, felt at least encouraged when we received the precious phial containing the serum, with instructions on how to take it. I sensed that he wanted to stay in Switzerland – which at least represented hope – and that the thought of returning to England depressed him.

My brother came out to help us on the last few days

of our stay because I was uneasy about attempting the return journey with Jacques alone.

At Geneva airport, Jacques looks extremely weak. Ten days of blood tests and waiting for Durovic's verdict have completely drained him. His haemoglobin is perilously low, and I am worried he will not survive the journey. My brother, Barry, walks up and down with him in the cold air just outside the airport lounge.

The customs officers are bolshie and won't let Barry through with us even to accompany Jacques in the wheelchair which took ages to arrive. On the plane Jacques' eyelids flicker, he is white and still and I keep looking at him, fearing he might expire. The withdrawal from morphine that Durovic recommended has affected him badly too, and I am not sure what I am seeing – withdrawal symptoms or a worsening condition generally.

To make matters worse, when we arrive at Heathrow, my sister-in-law cannot locate her car in the car park and we are left waiting for what seems an age with the feeling that everything is conspiring against us. How we both long to be back in crisp, comfortable Switzerland where it all seemed like a bad dream – instead of grey, comfortless England where the reality is only too apparent.

Jacques had not much longer to live, and this is my journal account of his last days, written in December 1987:

Jacques is so swollen around the middle,
unbalancing his whole gait, that the local
doctor thinks he should have some fluid
drained. He can scarcely breathe, walk or talk:
everything hurts – though he refuses to take
morphine but instead takes alarmingly large
doses of paracetamol and codeine alternately.

There was some dispute about whether or not to
drain the fluid – and it was decided to put Jacques into
hospital – which he had been resisting all along. In fact,
I had had to promise him early on I would nurse him
myself at home. He also disliked the idea of a hospice –
since it suggested to him that there was no hope left at
all. I could not fight this attitude – on the one hand, it
showed his enormous courage, on the other it made
for many complications. We hear much about the
'death with dignity' the hospice can offer – and indeed,
I have witnessed such deaths, but this can only apply
to those who accept the idea that there can be a
'preparation' for dying. For those who, like Jacques,
feel that as long as one draws breath there is a chance
for recovery and that one should battle to the end, the
hospice remains a very alien idea – and though the
battle itself may be a courageous and dignified one, the
death itself can be the opposite.

The NHS hospital was suffering at the time from lack
of funds and staff demoralization and simply could not
cope in a sufficiently sensitive way with a terminal
patient. The grimness of his surroundings compounded
his misery and my feelings of impotence. Since I did
not want to add to his distress I tried, desperately, to
get him moved into a more homely private clinic. It
took all my efforts to effect this and to have him
moved.

This is one of my last diary entries before Jacques died:

> On a Saturday afternoon I sit on his bed and we watch the first film Jacques ever saw in Vienna on the little portable television my brother Barry has brought – *Maytime* with Jeannette MacDonald and Nelson Eddy; and I weep as they sing 'Sweethearts', realizing this will probably be Jacques' last film. The circle is complete, I sit on the bed and hold his hand. Today we are at last moving to the private hospital: in one final great effort, I manage to get Jacques out into a taxi, after waiting in the rain for what seemed like ages. At last he is in a light and airy room with a view and can watch the birds fluttering around the bird table.

But Jacques' spirit and morale had finally gone, and he died the following day. His poor body could stand it no longer. My daughter Mina, who had broken off her studies in Manchester to come down to help nurse Jacques, stayed with me in the little hospital room where they had given us temporary beds. Richard, the extraordinarily caring nurse who had bathed and powdered him and tried to make him feel more comfortable, woke us in the middle of the night to break the news that Jacques' body had finally given way. Richard had dressed him in the new nightwear a friend had sent, and Mina and I both went to say our farewells.

'In the spring, in the spring', Jacques had sung so bravely on his final walks, but that spring had never come. I kept hearing the words of that song as my brother drove me home from the hospital, along the dark winding roads of Burnham Beeches. I remember the feeling I had in the car that night: 'I am alone, he is no longer there for me. There is no one between me and the world.' I was engulfed in a feeling of utter desolation.

Chapter Two

A Difficult Song

'This is like me singing a very difficult song and everyone else here is humming with me.'

Mourner

Mercifully most funerals are arranged by close relatives or friends, and the bereaved themselves, often feeling dazed and anaesthetized, somehow 'sleepwalk' through the whole event. Like most people I had absolutely no knowledge of how one sets about organizing a funeral: the costs, local authority laws, etc. Fortunately my brother Barry took over, though in common with many people I had a shock when I realized just how expensive a decent burial was. I have only vague memories of my brother and son, Elias, making a journey to the registrar's office, and coming home with a death certificate and telling me about the burial plot. I also had no idea that the office hours for the registration of deaths, or the necessity to do a post mortem, could delay a funeral for days (and Jewish law dictates that the burial should take place as soon as possible after the death). The bureaucracy can cause much anxiety, as can the chore of having to inform the world at large of what has happened. Again, I had no consciousness of who was doing this or how, though occasionally a name would occur to me of someone I felt had to be informed.

In my state of bewilderment and shock, I felt immense dread at having to go through the whole funeral rite: I dreaded too the thought of having to put my children through this ordeal. I felt so totally inexperienced and afraid of doing something wrong. I also felt unable to assert myself or express any wishes of my own since my head was not clear. I allowed myself, because I had no choice, to be *led* through the whole thing; and, as it happened, this allowing myself to be organized helped me – with the assistance of a very sympathetic minister – to gain a little confidence.

What I dreaded most was the public expression of my grief. As long as I could keep it to myself – my swollen eyes, frequent floods of tears, and shaky walk – I was all right: but the thought of letting the world see my grief appalled me. I couldn't make up my mind what to wear: that was my biggest dilemma that morning. Jews are not obliged to wear black, but the sombre mood nonetheless seems to dictate it. I decided to wear a black silk headscarf rather than a hat. I had organized dark clothes for my children the day before. This at least gave me something to focus on. I still recall wandering through the dress department of Marks and Spencer just after my father died, to pick out a suitable dress, as the only action which temporarily restored my sanity. At the funeral I was conscious only of my children flanking me on either side, each of us leaning on the other for support: of the heavy dark overcoat my son wore, making him look much older than his years, and my daughter's pale face, swollen from crying. I was conscious of us as a sort of tragic triad – the three of us seemed locked together into our tragedy – inseparable at that point. I followed the casket as if in a trance, although I remember picking out certain people with both surprise and gratitude . . . a friend arriving late with a baby in a pushchair . . . my mother's white hair under her headscarf. I went through all the motions of the funeral in a complete daze. It was as if a drum were beating a rhythm and leading me forward. I just followed until finally I threw some earth on the grave with my bare hands, shook hands with everyone, and trance-like, was led back home again in my brother's big, smooth, comfortable car.

I don't think there is any advice one can give on how to get through the ordeal of the funeral, except to say that you will get through it somehow. Mercifully you will be numb: even your physical movements will seem to be happening elsewhere. You will lean on somebody – and somehow be carried along. Remember that you are allowed to be whatever you are, there are no 'standards'. Your friends will be there to buoy you up: not to remark on your swollen red eyes, or lack of composure. Everyone *wants* to be composed, to add dignity and solemnity to the event – but if you do break down it is not the end of the world. Don't expect too much of yourself.

If you don't know him already, it is certainly helpful to acquaint yourself with the minister who will be officiating on this painful day, to get some idea of what will happen. I remember that I was terribly worried at the thought of not knowing what to do – what was expected of me – and I was grateful to be given a sort of outline of procedure earlier in the day. Although initially reluctant, as he grew weaker Jacques had been willing to receive visits from the local rabbi. I think in the beginning he saw these visits as a sign that his days were numbered, that he had been given up, and he did not want to acknowledge this; but as time went on and he was more reconciled to, though not passively accepting of, his own possible death, he could face the rabbi with less fear and dread. I myself was greatly comforted by his visits. It was he too who gave the children and me the courage to get through the funeral by explaining what would happen at every stage, and above all, stressing that these rites were meant to comfort the mourner. The bereaved so often feel at a loss in this area and somehow the rules give them something to hang on to. I consulted him on every aspect of mourning rites. Was it all right for me to wear this? What sort of wording did one put on the headstone? What did one do when visiting the cemetery?

It is also a good idea to talk to your minister about the person you have lost – his interests, passions and the major events in his life – so that whoever officiates at the funeral is thoroughly acquainted with the 'essence' of the man and any speech he makes will have a personal ring about it. Jacques and his paintings were inseparable. It was his talent that had persuaded his art teacher in occupied Vienna to help get him a place on one of the last children's trains: through all the turbulent years of his disrupted youth his talent and will to paint had been a flaming beacon. Later on he had dozens of one-man shows around the world, and his paintings hung in many major museums and galleries. Although largely a landscape painter he had become known, too, as one of the finest portrait painters in the United States. So it was right that the minister conducting the funeral should address himself to the public man – the artist – as well as to the husband and father we had lost. Deciding the balance however was not easy – and I was grateful to have a minister who managed to incorporate both into the very moving and sensitive address he gave by the grave. The last public statement about the man is very important to all widows – and I have heard some express dismay and disappointment because the last few words spoken were ill chosen. Most want public recognition of some kind; private emotions come later.

In the Jewish religion there is a traditional week of mourning – the *Shiva* – ('shiva' being the Hebrew word for seven). During this period a brief evening service is held in the mourner's home and the mourners themselves sit on low stools receiving visitors. I had been dreading this too. It is said to be comforting for the mourners to receive streams of visitors paying their respects. All food is prepared elsewhere and brought for the mourners, partly as a sign of their 'taboo' state and partly to free them from domestic chores.

I have a vague memory of the clatter of cups and saucers and of people chatting as the cake was handed round; of hearing the same comments repeated; 'Time will heal' – 'At least you have your children' – 'It's good that you have your work' – 'You're still young' – 'Life must go on'. I also remember being touched by the number of far-flung old school friends and friends of my children who bothered to come. It felt like a whole network of support had somehow been garnered, making me aware that I was part of a community – that they, too, would feel the loss and somehow try to plug the hole left. In fact the Shiva turned out to be much more reassuring than I had anticipated. For one thing it gave me a focus for each day. Otherwise those early days would undoubtedly have seemed infinitely grey and formless: but I knew I had to get up and get dressed and make myself fairly presentable. The important thing, looking back on it now, was that there was something to do, even if it was only arranging myself on the low stool and waiting. I am a great believer that much of life consists in 'something to do': that with the first sign of outer formlessness, inner chaos starts to reign. After the second day, I actually started to look forward to seeing certain people: I was beginning to appreciate that their presence was a comfort to me. It seemed to have the same effect on my children, who had also been dreading it.

Recently, I heard a young mourner talking on a television programme about the loss of a baby, describing the effects of having people around soon after the death: 'Even in the absolute pit of grief, healing began. Family and friends gathered around us – it was wonderful. I recounted and recounted again to all those people what had happened: I sifted it all. Just listening – holding our hands – being with us – that was a huge thing. It allowed us to get it into our own heads. We just *were* . . . we allowed ourselves to grieve.'

By the end of the week, when we'd heard the same expressions over and over again – when I had explained for what seemed like the thousandth time exactly how Jacques' illness had been diagnosed, and how the death had occurred (for the Shiva forces you to talk about these things), I felt drained, but somehow minimally better, as if I had purged something from my system. And my fear of facing people had at least passed, although I was far from ready to face the world again. I would say that while it does exert some unwelcome pressures on the mourner, the Shiva is a valuable thing both allowing you 'time out' before you go into the world again and giving you the necessary recognition of your state of mind, which is very important. It has been said that the English have forgotten how to grieve. It is only in very rare cases that mourners can say goodbye to the body or are encouraged to touch, hold, kiss or photograph it, all of which may bring comfort. The emphasis is on 'private grief', which is a very lonely experience – but the only one considered respectable. The normal English response (and one I have often encountered) is to say 'Yes, you must do your crying, but preferably not in front of me, in case it seems that I am the one who has caused your tears – rather than the death itself.'

In other societies like India they do have a blueprint for mourning. People are encouraged to hold the hand of the dead person during the funeral, there is a lot of touching and crying in public, as well as a lot of 'repeating' of how the death happened. Similarly the Jewish Shiva, where there is precisely this repeating, this retelling of the tale, of all the details of the illness and the death, does provide catharsis, as does the Irish wake, or the traditional Caribbean funeral and mourning rites, where there is a lot of family support and talking. In England one is made to feel that death and mourning are something to be shoved under the carpet – a 'disease', a 'temporary hiccup' to be recovered from as soon as possible. But the bereaved don't immediately wish to be told to 'get on with your life'. Sooner or later life will take over, but when you are feeling more like weeping, wailing and having hysterics why should you get on with your life? More likely all you can do at this point, as my counsellor said, is 'crawl around at the bottom'.

After Jacques' death our rabbi continued to visit us for several weeks, and was especially helpful when my daughter went through a severe 'crisis of grief', leaving me feeling useless and anxious. I personally found it easier at that stage to open up to a minister who had known all our family for years, than to a bereavement counsellor – though in fact this particular rabbi had been trained as a counsellor. I had religious needs and feelings and had to express them. We talked a lot about suffering and the Jewish attitude to it, which is very different from the Christian one. I was particularly struck by this when sometime later I went to see the play _Shadowlands_, which tells the story of the relationship between the writer C. S. Lewis and an American, Joy Davidman, whom he met and fell in love with late in his life and who died of cancer. Its message had deep meaning for me at that particular time as this diary extract shows:

> _Shadowlands_ proved deeply upsetting. Frail Jane Lapotaire looked so much like a cancer victim – as she lay in her bed, centre stage, and Nigel Hawthorne showed all the 'angst' of the closely involved relative. It brought back so many painful memories (especially the scene in the hotel where the couple had attempted to snatch a few days' holiday in one of her remissions). The Christian view on suffering expressed by C. S. Lewis is that 'pain is God's megaphone to a deaf world', that this life is merely the Shadowland. This is not the Jewish one – which in one sense is fortunate: for Judaism which is so much more 'this worldly' does not have suffering at the centre, though it does give one compensation for suffering in the same sense that Christianity

does. We have only the knowledge that our pain may be the result of our fathers' or forefathers' sins – but not that it serves any positive function or enables us in any way. It is there – as the story of Job shows – to test our faith in God and to show us how little we are capable of understanding His mysterious ways. I sensed it was very comforting to have a play which gave suffering pain and death a meaning on our West End stage. One felt the sense of release in the audience, who gave it a standing ovation. Perhaps this was the closest we'd get in our day and age to a public psychodrama, a ritual expressing grief.

The role of religion in bereavement varies from person to person. If it has always been a central feature of your life, it is obviously going to play a great part in death. But I have known those who have never stepped inside a church or synagogue, who would claim to be total non-believers or atheists, find comfort in some simple words of prayer or ritual following their first loss. Faced with death, the ultimate chaos or collapse of structure, it is human to look for meaning – unless, of course, one is so angry with one's God (this can happen, particularly in the case of someone who has nursed the terminally ill) that rejection of everything religious is the only response.

I do not think I could have coped with the crisis of Jacques' illness and his eventual death without the help of religion. I grew to rely increasingly on my own private prayers, and especially on readings from the book of Psalms which I kept – and still keep – at all times on the table beside my bed. I remember Anatoly

Scharansky, the Soviet dissident, telling me in an interview that he could not have got through his long years of imprisonment in the Soviet Union without his own little book of Psalms, which he kept continually by him. I know why he found the Psalms particularly comforting and encouraging: there is one for every mood – ranging from the sad to the triumphant and defiant. I would read them out loud to Jacques during his illness, and each night we chose one at random just by opening the page, which we would see as having a special significance on that day.

Until his illness Jacques had not been religious in the formal sense, although he believed deeply that God spoke to him, made His presence known, through his art, and that evidence of God was all around in nature itself. It was only during the terminal stages of his illness that he started to pray with me and listen to the Psalms, and it became a major part of his personal battle against the disease. For myself I know that I could not have got through the nights immediately preceding and following his death without my little book of Psalms and my constant prayers.

Chapter Three

· Shadowland

*'Time was not measured out in hours or by lightness and dark,
grief had a time of its own, and a rhythm, so that she was either
weeping over some particular memory, or craving for his
physical body . . . '*

Susan Hill, *In the Springtime of the Year*

The first few weeks after the funeral went in a haze. I
was vaguely aware of people coming and going, of
letters of condolence pouring in every day. Of the
phone calls (fortunately I had installed an answering
machine during Jacques' illness to take some of the
pressure off, for I didn't have the energy or the
inclination to field the calls), of the meals which were
put in front of me by my mother who stayed for an
extra week. It was very much like being a convalescent
– having 'time out'. I made no demands whatsoever on
myself: I was thoroughly cocooned. I know that many
are forced to go right back into the world again but in
those early days I didn't venture out of the house at all.
When I did go even for a five-minute walk in our little
lane I'd be reminded of the nightly walks Jacques, I and
the children had taken together in the last few weeks
of his life. It was too painful, so I would return home.
The family were gathered around me and I was
becoming increasingly aware of, and anxious about
their emotions, although unable physically even to
venture off the couch and find the initiative to make a
cup of tea. I would sit for hours inert, yet somewhere in
the back of my mind was the terrifying thought that
sooner or later this limbo would have to end and I

would have to start answering the bills and letters and venturing out to the shops and organizing my life.

For weeks after Jacques' death I felt reduced to a shadow. I couldn't even go shopping, for above all I had the feeling that I must avoid anybody who had known me before. I experienced a mixture of shame and self consciousness at the mere fact that I still existed. I have heard others talk of this shame. I tried to remain invisible, and although not obliged by religion to wear black, I still chose to dress in dark colours. When eventually I walked a few hundred yards down the road to the shops I skulked in doorways, scared even to catch my reflection in a window. I wondered if people could *see* I was a widow? My first feelings were of such terrible vulnerability that I would only talk to those I felt sure would not, even by a simple thoughtless word, bruise me any further. This feeling of exposure and rawness is so powerful in the early days of bereavement that one widow spoke of the feeling of walking around without any skin when she first went out.

When my mother had gone and I was finally left alone in the big old house (the children had returned to college), my first reaction was to run away, to jump on a plane to Spain, South America, Australia - anywhere. I craved sunlight, as I seemed to be enveloped in greyness. I realized however that I was far too frail to go anywhere; I felt dizzy merely entering a supermarket. My second reaction was to shut myself within my own four walls. My house was a comfort to me; anything familiar was a comfort. I couldn't understand it when people asked almost immediately, 'Are you moving?' Why should I want to move? One trauma at a time was enough. So I stayed put, attempting only the most minor tasks. Even watering the plants seemed to take hours now; while putting on the kettle was a task of gargantuan proportions.

Death gives one a strange sense of catastrophe – the feeling that the world is no longer controllable – that because of one's fragility anything can happen to anyone at any time. This fearfulness took a long time to come to terms with. It was to return every time I suffered a loss: I went into total panic for example when my cat was run over. Meanwhile, as everyone keeps reminding you, 'life has to go on' – which is not easy when one is feeling the terrible inertia, numbness or depression of the early grief. It is precisely at that time that one seems to be hit by the demands that the life that has to go on makes – especially if, like me, through coping with illness you have not worked for six months and the household has been entirely neglected. Many widows speak of the difficulty of those early weeks when, depleted of all energy, they have to cope with getting some order into their practical affairs. This is when one really craves some help, and any offer of assistance with everyday chores at this point is immensely valuable.

In my frail physical state I was suffering without realizing it classic 'panic attack' symptoms. I was relieved to read in Lily Pincus' book, *Death in the Family*, that people often fracture bones and fall over after bereavement because they 'lose their sense of balance'. I suffered terrible dizziness in those first few months. It would invariably happen to me in the same spot; I only had to walk down the road and go into Marks and Spencer, and I would keel over. I was convinced I had contracted something like Meunier's Disease, or worse. My doctor gave me Stemotil, which is routinely given for middle ear infection and loss of balance, and it did help. At one point I was convinced I had developed a heart problem, and was having all the classic symptoms of a heart attack. But my bereavement counsellor explained that my palpitations and irregular heartbeat were due to extreme anxiety. It was, of course, a 'broken heart' problem which resulted in all the pounding and irregularity. Since my world had been turned upside down was it any wonder I felt so unbalanced? As I gradually regained control over my life the anxiety and the symptoms subsided.

It is not surprising that many widows tend to get ill after their bereavement, since they neglect themselves physically. Weight loss, even anorexia, is extremely common. Not only does depression take away the appetite, but shopping and cooking for one is at first very strange. It takes some time to adjust to quantities and the bleak experience of eating alone. I realized after a couple of months that my clothes were hanging off me and that I had lost almost two stone. It was scarcely surprising, since I hardly shopped. I then decided that even if I didn't have any appetite I would force myself to eat a little. Increasingly aware of all my new responsibilities I suddenly felt that I must make sure I kept my health and energy, because there was only me and no one else to keep everything going. I also found out that taking extra care with diet and exercise in itself helps give a structure to one's life and prevents depression. I started once again to stick to Leslie Kenton's 50% 'raw energy' diet, taking a mineral and vitamin supplement, running once a week (though at first I scarcely ran around the block) and doing a very minimal daily exercise routine (mainly stretch exercises based on ballet). It all helped to give

me a sense of purpose and a feeling that I was
somebody worth doing these things for. At this stage
feelings of low self-esteem, even worthlessness, are
very common and anything that can make you cherish
yourself again is a step in the right direction.

In those early days my need for sanctuary was great.
Outside the house I felt vulnerable; inside, on home
ground, I could talk, listen, smile and act like a fairly
normal human being. Above all, I could be myself. This
'self' would often be an infantile one – the one I
regressed to – and sometimes I felt about three years
old, as I sat there on the big couch cuddling my cats,
the only comfort I could find. It was different outside,
where I was open to abuse at any time and where in
the most unexpected places and at the most unlikely
times, and often when I felt that things were going
well, the smallest reminder would bring the most raw
and savage emotions rushing to the surface. It could be
anything, an item I saw in a shop window that
reminded me of something we had bought together, or
a smell, or a sound. I remember being particularly
upset passing a beautiful lingerie shop in town where
Jacques had always bought me my birthday presents –
the sort of beautiful crepe de chine luxury underwear
that I would never dream of buying myself and would
possibly never have anyone else buy me again. I
rushed home and looked at it wrapped in tissue in my
drawers – a lot of it still unworn – and wept out of sheer
guilt for not having worn it when he was alive.

'You must have time to mourn,' people say piously.
What do they mean? All too often they imply that you
are incapable of sorting out your own emotions and
need to see a 'professional'. But I see this as a

distraction from the real business of mourning.

Today, 'bereavement counselling' is often recommended almost as a sort of panacea for grief. I would
not hesitate to advise bereavement counselling for
those who feel they need it, but I do believe that
because of the way we have medicalized death, and
because of our taboo on 'mourning' (in the sense that
the Victorians used to mourn), we have tended to
shove this whole area of responsibility on to the
professionals. Sending someone off for immediate
bereavement counselling lets everyone else off the
hook. We compartmentalize death, just as we do life.
The average person is so ill at ease with death and the
mourner, that he has nothing to say to them: hence the
discomfiture and avoidance and tendency to try to
'normalize' the mourner as soon as possible. The
admiring phrase so often applied to mourners, 'Isn't
she coping well?' means in fact, 'Isn't she coping well
by not making us feel uncomfortable?'

While not underestimating the value of counsellors,
I would begin with the question: 'How does one start
to come to terms with the worst of the numbness and
depression using *one's own inner resources*? Here,
perhaps, a counsellor can point the way; but it is far
better, I think, to encourage people to believe they
have it *within them* to cope and make progress. Like any
journey or process the point of departure is very
important. If I had to name one thing which helped me
come to terms with the very raw feelings in the early
days of my bereavement I would say 'dreams' and the
experience I had with 'dream therapy'. Admittedly I
had used it for several years in other contexts. I am a
great believer that just about anything can serve as a
therapy: that one does not *necessarily* need professional

bereavement counsellors: that a good friend or informal support group can serve very much the same purpose – though I do believe that when a person is 'stuck' in their grief, blocked in some way, a catalyst or 'enabler' of some sort is needed. Very often counselling is done by other widows who provide the support of shared experience. This is the sort of support the national organization CRUSE offers to the recently bereaved. CRUSE is an organization founded for widows and named after the biblical story of the widow with the miraculous cure of oil. At CRUSE a widow can talk over her problems. They operate a referral system and there is a monthly newsletter to which a widow can subscribe. The nearest branch can be found in the telephone directory. I know many who have benefited from it, though I did not use it myself. Other people who have been bereaved at least can say, 'I know how you feel' and mean it. A support group of this kind can be invaluable and today I help on one myself – but you have to be ready for it.

The timing of counselling is all-important. Grief counselling I feel would have little meaning in the early days when you are numb, confused and without the will to communicate or share the experience. The first step needed here is to know exactly what you *are* feeling: to put yourself in touch with your sadness, fear and feelings. Later, I am sure that groups of many kinds can be very helpful – but in the early days there is much to be said for staying cloistered and turning inwards, if that is what you want.

Like nothing else, bereavement forces you to come to terms with your inner life: you either face up to what is in your psyche or turn to other distractions – drink, drugs, or even promiscuity – to act as a temporary 'anaesthetic'. It has never been more important to know what is going on in your subconscious. Freud always held that the 'Royal Road' to the subconscious was through dreams. Ever since I trained as a Gestalt therapist in the US almost twenty years ago I have used dreams and 'dream workshop' techniques to sort out many dilemmas.

I am convinced that working with dreams can be enormously beneficial in coming to terms with grief or loss of any kind, and that they provide not only a guide to what is happening in our subconscious but a key, too, to the way forward – and that is the important thing. I am a firm believer that an answer of some kind always lies hidden in a dream, a way ahead to the future, and that by working with that dream, remembering, writing it down, 'living' with it in your waking hours, you will somehow find some of life's knots unravelling themselves. This, I feel, is absolutely crucial when trying to emerge from that familiar 'grey fog' that so many people describe following a bereavement.

Many people find soon after a death that they have quite startling dreams in which the dead person appears as if alive, in a very vivid way that can either be a source of great distress or great comfort – sometimes both. I myself had several very powerful dreams soon after both my father and Jacques died. When I could, I would write them down immediately. It is quite common to dream that the dead person has returned or been made well.

Journal entry, 5 July 1988

Every once in a while Jacques comes back to me in a dream. These dreams have a different feel from other dreams, and are so vivid that it is tempting to feel that the dead really are making themselves known to you from some other dimension in time. I am always left in almost a 'hang-over' state after one of these dreams when I appear to go into a very deep sleep, feeling almost anaesthetized. Some people never apparently experience these dreams – these are often people who are almost frightened to experience deep feeling, as for instance the widow who told me she would be scared to dream of a dead person. Many people still retain a remarkably super-stitious attitude towards dreams – much of it perhaps reflecting a guilt which they have failed to come to terms with. I have always cherished my dreams, knowing they always contain the key to some missing element in my life, and invariably I have found that I will have one almost immediately after someone close to me has died. Whether this is because I am very aware of my dreams or for some other reason, I do not know.

This one took place in a West End department store (perhaps Liberty – as there was lots of dark wood and narrow stairways everywhere). In it, I ran into a woman friend (a very well-to-do one) who at first looked the other way. I then made an approach and said, 'It is not what you think: Jacques has come

back for a short time to be with me, he is here
now, shopping.' And lo and behold, a very
pale and obviously ill Jacques appeared. We
made him sit down in a chair. I told the friend
that he had been through hell the night
before, but that all would be well once he got
back to heaven. There were then a few flashes
of scenes from the previous night, with
Jacques sweating it out in what appeared to
be some sort of torture chamber . . .

I remember that I was left feeling very sad and
uneasy and with strong feeling of hang-over when I
awoke. I decided to visit the cemetery after picking a
few flowers from the garden. I chose the few precious
sweet-peas I'd grown myself from seed – which was
significant since I'd always grown the special flowers
Jacques liked to paint. There was a sense of continuity
in still arranging the colours for him. At the cemetery I
arranged the flowers in the small glass vase I kept
there, and pulled up the weeds and long grass that had
grown up around the grave: I had not visited for some
weeks. As I did this I struck up a conversation with a
young woman attending her mother's grave nearby.
This was the first time I had found someone else doing
the same thing, and it gave me a feeling of comfort and
commiseration.

With this particular dream, it was the feeling that
lingered afterwards that bothered me, and it took me a
while to recognize what was causing it – the feelings of
guilt and wretchedness over Jacques' illness . . . the
feeling of social isolation, and the sadness that certain
people had cut me out of their lives, which in my
supersensitive state seemed to indicate that they were

blaming me for something. The fact that I visited the cemetery showed I wanted to re-open a dialogue as it were, find some kind of solution. The dream had made me take that action, though the meaning was not immediately apparent.

Every dream left its own flavour, sadnesses and sometimes comfort, and it often took some time for its meaning to become apparent. Only when I had tossed the dreams around in my own mind, did I understand what they were telling me – and only then could I see them as stepping stones to a way forward. I believe that recalling dreams in the bereavement process has not been widely commented upon, except in the context of psycho-analysis, and I am not here proposing interpretations along any orthodox lines – either Freudian, Jungian or anything else. I do not believe that there can be a fixed interpretation for the symbols that appear in our dreams. Only the dreamer can know what they mean in the context of our whole life, past, present and future. I would resent anyone superimposing meaning on *my* dreams – telling me *that* is what it means. It often takes a very long time for the meaning to emerge and when it does, it may not be the meaning you immediately credited it with.

In dreaming you have a chance not only to locate lost parts of yourself – but to find ways of repairing the holes. Dreams have a wisdom. Dreams allow you to get in touch, to start a conversation with your psyche. Carl Jung spoke of something he called 'active imagination', which was 'the art of letting things happen'. 'We must be able to let things happen in the psyche,' he wrote. He was interested in what happened when the mind was left to its own devices, so to speak, without any of the usual guidance or bullying by the ego. He called this 'the natural mind' – best seen in fantasy. In sleep, fantasy of course takes the form of dreams. It can happen in waking life too – where we continue to dream below the threshold of consciousness. Jung devised a technique whereby he could get himself into a state of 'reverie' – half-way between sleep and waking. He did it by imagining he was descending into a cave. I do it when I am in a drowsy state at night lying in bed by imagining I am swimming underwater: this always seems to provoke an unusually vivid dream. Jung insisted that all the figures that emerge from either dreams or reverie must be treated as actual experiences, as real people. If we work with them hard and long enough we realize that instead of deriving them from our psychic state, we derive our psychic state from them. This is why the mood and feelings of a dream seem to linger, and why it is important to work out exactly what experiences the figures in our dreams stand for.

Dream deprivation, I believe, can be one of the prime causes of depression. I also believe that much insomnia is caused by this rather than anything physical – that people have not been given the chance to sort through the symbols of the mind. I know that as soon as I dream deeply and vividly I sleep well too. People who say that they never ever dream are generally lacking in any kind of self-awareness, which is the first step to health and reparation; it can be worth more than all the intensive long-term therapy in the world, if used in the right way. Since bereavement means an enormous hole torn in the personality, and necessitates building anew, I suggest that the dream is a very good place from which to start. And if, like me, you often go to sleep quite easily but wake up at dawn with an over-active mind, you may find, as I do, that making yourself a hot drink and a sandwich helps you to drift back into sleep and can promote quite vivid dreams just before waking, easily remembered.

Keep a notebook and pen by the side of your bed, and even if you just remember a fragment of the dream, this gives you something to work on. Jot down whatever you remember of the dream as soon as possible – as dreams, however vivid, tend to fade very rapidly. Start the day with your 'dreamwork', take a few minutes to simplify and digest what was in the dream. Above all try to remember the feeling it gave you. Was it fear, joy, guilt, anger, regret, tenderness, relief? Since every part of the dream was, in a sense, a part of yourself, try to act out each part. Allow yourself to wallow in the feelings left over from the dream: in those feelings lies the way ahead – for all dreams contain solutions to the problems you are trying to solve or resolve in your life. Take yourself again, again and again, step by step through what you remember of the dream. Note especially the sequences – where one part ends, and a new scene begins. If the dream ended abruptly, try to imagine where it was leading.

Remembering dreams takes practice. You will find it becomes easier. You will find too that once you start dreaming you may have several nights of particularly vivid dreams and then an apparent dearth. Regard your 'dreamwork' as a healing process. Transformations are taking place within you: be thankful for the dreams. They are your inner wisdom – your best guide for your own happiness and the key to creativity. Each dream will bring you one step further along the path to recovery.

Dreaming, of course, is part of your normal sleep

pattern, but one of the problems I had, in common with many people who have been bereaved or are in a very agitated state, was a severe sleep disorder. My normal sleep patterns had been disturbed when Jacques became seriously ill and I had to be acutely sensitive to his needs in the night – waking up every hour or so. I also had to have almost super-human energy by day to cope with both the nursing and keeping up his morale. After a while I realized that unless I slept at night I would be a wreck by day, unable to meet those needs. I therefore arranged at one point for somebody else to take over the night nursing, and asked my doctor for a light sleeping pill: I knew that a good night's rest was crucial and I also knew that apart from anything else, the level of anxiety I was experiencing would never enable me to achieve it normally.

My doctor prescribed Temazepam, which he assured me would 'tip me into sleep', was perfectly safe, and would have no after effects – unlike the old barbiturates. What he did not tell me was that, in common with all tranquillizers, it was highly addictive, and that once I started to come off it I would have severe withdrawal symptoms. I now know that many of the symptoms such as dizziness, palpitations and night sweats that I attributed to anxiety, panic and depression in the early days were actually due to my attempting to come off Temazepam unsupervised. Apart from the disturbed sleep patterns I would invariably wake in the middle of the night and start to panic about everything. It was only when I mentioned it to a psychiatrist friend who happened to specialize in sleep disorders that he suggested the Temazepam might be to blame – and told me that one can become addicted to this group of drugs in as little as a week. Few doctors however point this out to their patients, who can be left with very distressing withdrawal symptoms which only add to their state of anxiety. My doctor friend recommended a special 'withdrawal pack' available from some pharmaceutical firms which gradually cuts the dose over a period of eight weeks. This worked reasonably well – it did minimize unpleasant symptoms – but it still left me unable to sleep for more than two or three hours at a spell. As I felt that sleep was essential to my being able to function at all, I took myself off to see the hypnotherapist who had acted as my bereavement counsellor. She proved tremendously helpful – not only in restoring my sleep patterns and lowering my anxiety, but also enabling me to find reserves of energy and courage within myself which I never thought I had.

'Get out of the house,' urged friends. 'Take a trip.' Distractions, always distractions. This seemed to be other people's solution. In theory it was very appealing, though in my state of hesitancy, uncertainty, I could hardly bring myself to make such a major decision and it took several changes of mind and cancelled airline bookings before I finally committed myself to a four-day trip to Paris to see some relatives.

I could only risk visiting 'safe' places – and Paris was one of them. My cousins there were warm and welcoming: there were prolonged meals, lots of coffee drinking and their 'carte blanche' to all the major art exhibitions. I went from one to another. I have never been very good at absorbing paintings at exhibitions – and now I forced myself to keep on the move. For twelve hours a day I dragged myself from Le Petit

Palais to Le Grand Palais; from Le Musée d'Orsay to
the Centre Pompidou. My eyes and feet could scarcely
cope with any more, but I was forcing myself to look
outwards, to try at least to focus on hundreds of
paintings even if I only really took in one or two. I had
always looked at paintings with Jacques and this was
some kind of bid to encompass the whole art world in
one sweep – a giddying attempt to exorcize all the
paintings we had ever seen or discussed together. It
was as if I felt compelled to look at them, to understand
their essence in order to make some sense of my own
experience.

Then it happened: I had been walking around all
day and it was cold. Tired and hungry, I stopped to eat
a pancake at a small crêperie in the Ile St Louis. I had
hardly taken the first bite when the tears came
flooding. Jacques and I had eaten crêpes together on
our last trip to Paris. I looked into a mirror and saw my
own reflection: in my mind's eye I saw two people –
but the solitary figure there told me I was alone.
Desolate, I told my cousins I wanted to go home.

In an attempt to cheer me up they gave me an Yves
Saint Laurent silk scarf in vibrant purple, green and
red. The colours were so alive, they raised my spirits a
little. Until then I had worn dark colours: now I dared
to drape the brilliant scarf round my neck – a small but
important concession.

Once home, I realized my trip to Paris had at least
restored a little confidence. If I could get on a plane, I
could phone some of my editors and colleagues, and at
least establish contact again. I hadn't worked for
almost six months and there were mounting debts to
face. I had to make a start somewhere, and I decided
that rather than sell the house, and face uprooting

myself at this stage, I would work flat out and somehow pay off our debts myself.

It was my first major decision. Fortunately I had built up a career over twenty or so years and could, if I applied myself to it, make a living wage. There are many women of course, who are not equipped to do so, who can scarcely manage on a widow's pension and are forced to sell their houses to pay their husband's debts as well as keep themselves. Making those early phone calls, deciding to work again, was the hardest step I had to take. But the realization that some part of me – the professional part – lived on, was to make an enormous difference to my recovery. Paris then had done the trick: it had made me see, at least, what my main priorities were: and at that time they were staying in the home I loved, and in order to do so, starting to find my way back into the world of journalism again.

Chapter Four

Those Manilla Envelopes

'Work was my way out. Four days after the funeral I decided to honour a contract that would take me away for nine weeks, doing a show in a different town every night. I don't remember a thing about that period of my life, where I went, what I did.'
Katie Boyle

While I'm aware that not everyone has a career or even a job to fall back on, there is no doubt that one of the best strategies for coping with bereavement, and especially the loss of identity and structure which follows, is getting involved in work of some kind. In my case, work proved an absolute godsend. Without it, I might have found it impossible to rebuild the structure of my days, to regain confidence, and above all, to meet my financial commitments. Having to focus on something outside of one's own immediate feelings and problems is not only a kind of anaesthetic, but a spur, a springboard for action. It becomes almost an entire *raison d'être*. As a columnist and feature writer I had to break myself in gently: in the early stages I had completely lost confidence even about my writing and for a short time believed I would never do it again. It was only when editors and colleagues offered me commissions that were well within my range for that time, and showed particular under-standing, that I slowly began to write again. My first pieces were on widowhood itself, which both allowed me to express urgent feelings and to feel that I was communicating something useful. I did not attempt my *Daily Mail* television column (which requires a certain sparkiness) for some months: I did know however, that the minute I saw my by-line in the paper, I felt more cheerful that day. This is my journal entry at the time columnist Jean Rook lost her husband, I particularly identified with one thing Jean had written:

'When I read the column, I knew I was still Jean Rook of the *Daily Express*.'

How well I know that feeling. Perhaps it's sad that it should take my photo and by-line to confirm that I am still there – still have an identity – but it does. On column days I leap out of bed about 7 a.m. and rush downstairs to see what they have done with the headlining and layout. I read it through a few times over a cup of tea to see what they have cut out, or changed – and if I'm pleased with what I see I feel a sense of elation, almost excitement all day – to see myself there and know not only that I still exist, still function, that I am still effective in the world in some way.

Work has continued to be a life-saver: I found myself capable of producing much more than I had ever imagined possible, partly because I do tend to fill the long and empty hours with writing of all sorts – from letters to journal entries, from my television columns to outlines of television programmes. One of my more bizarre strategies for coping with bereavement in the first year was attempting to write a sit-com about three generations of single women and their relationships with men – *Stepping Out*. It was based of course on my own rather unusual circumstances – having a mother also recently widowed, who'd started to 'date' again and who, in fact, had found herself a new partner – plus a daughter who had just set herself up in a partnership with someone she had known since school. I was in the odd position of having to worry about both of them, and of giving my own mother, who had suddenly become as girlish and coquettish as a teenager, advice.

Even on my blackest days I couldn't help appreciating the funny side of this situation and each day would put it all down in my sit-com. Someone once said that you can write your way out of anything – including hell. I was soon to discover the truth of this as I wrote my first black comedy, which I finally plucked up enough courage to show, in outline, to Linda Agran, then head of drama at London Weekend Television. She told me she thought that it had potential and I was about to take it to the next stage when, lo and behold, a new TV series was announced based on radio's *After Henry*, which used a very similar theme; and so my project had to be put on ice. I was naturally disappointed but at least it had served the purpose of enabling me to express – even exorcize – certain feelings through humour. I would spend two or three hours a day on it for a whole year and I am quite sure it was getting something out of my system.

For those who don't work it can be more difficult to find a new structure and routine in their lives. Some, like one young widow I know called Sarah – who was left financially secure but had never worked in her twenty-two years of marriage – find it in doing voluntary work and in new hobbies. She started to help out at the local hospice and to sing in the church choir. Others, like an elderly widow, Marie, find it through increased participation with their families.

Marie now looks after her grandchildren two or three days a week, and regularly travels north to see her other children. Other older widows are not so fortunate: Louise, seventy-nine, arthritic and with no family to speak of, is now after ten years of widowhood largely confined to her small flat – and has to rely on neighbours for shopping or outings. Fortunately her local church has a support network for widows like herself and sends a young woman as a home-help twice a week. Louise is also picked up and taken to a cards evening for the elderly.

Isolation and loneliness are the biggest problems that widows like Louise face. Poverty is another – especially for the young widow with children who has either been left in debt or without any means and is ill-equipped to work. She faces the poverty of many single parents. The more resourceful sometimes manage to retrain and start small businesses, or find self-employment – like driving a cab, running a small catering business, or creating artwork of some kind. Some who have never worked find themselves inheriting their husband's business and are determined to make a success of it. Twice Business Woman Of The Year, Jennifer Goldstein, head of J J Fashions, found herself in that situation when widowed in her early thirties. She went on to build a small business into one of the most successful ventures of the eighties.

All but the most wealthy and well provided for suffer some reduction in their standard of living which is inevitable when the chief wage earner dies. Unlike the single parent who has often chosen to be single *voluntarily*, the widow first has to accept the inevitability of what has happened to her before she can begin to find strategies to cope with the new reality – and acceptance may be the biggest step of all.

For me the early days were very much trial and error. I was in a state of constant worry about finances and work and felt I could take nothing for granted. It was only about two years after Jacques' death that my financial affairs started to fall into place. It is a mistake to believe that you can settle all of them immediately.

'Financial advisors' abound, though from my own experience I feel one should steer clear of them at first. I was persuaded to go to a very fancy firm of 'financial management consultants', but could not relate to them at all. I looked at their Mayfair penthouse suite and the glib salesman and it seemed to me that they were predators, waiting to get my non-existent money. In common with many of these firms they tried to persuade me to borrow far in excess of what I needed, which made me feel even more insecure. I was hardly surprised to learn two years later that they had been charged with fraud and misuse of funds. Something had made me hold back – either intuition or a puritanical streak. 'People like you never get rich,' the salesman had thrown at me. Perhaps not – but I felt mightily relieved not to have allowed myself to get carried away at the time. A year or so later, I could handle both my emotions and my finances with far greater objectivity. It often takes about a year, or at least six months, to know how you stand financially. You are not immediately able to assess your own potential income (especially if you're self employed or freelancing) or whether, as in my case, you will either want to or be able to step up productivity to boost your income (in my case I worked fiendishly hard to double it). This is why I feel it is often useless to do a 'projected income' report. How on earth do you know?

I was glad I waited before I made any major decisions – and then, having consulted my bank, my solicitor and an accountant, I was able to shop around for the best kind of investments and loans. What I learned above all is that as long as you are paying off part of your debt on a regular basis you can keep everyone happy – including, above all, yourself.

It's not unusual for widows of my generation to have to learn what any nineteen-year-old automatically knows today. I had been almost a 'child bride', as I had gone straight from my father's home to my husband's – and as Jacques was much older he was already used to handling finances himself. I had always thought that I was the only woman who had not been exposed to handling money, serious money, like mortgages, before I was widowed. So I was surprised to learn just how many women – even working ones with decent salaries – leave all the major money matters to their partners: bill paying, invoicing, dealing with insurance and banking. Money is a great source of anger and anxiety to the widow: all widows worry about it – whether they have been provided for or not (and many haven't). Many counsellors hold that anger over money is one of the greatest contributory causes to pathological grieving. I am convinced that women have special problems with money. This is not only because of their attitude towards it, which is a remarkably different one from the male approach – especially their perception of debt and credit which often send them into a panic – but because often they have never had any, or have handed over whatever they have had to their partner or put it in the family kitty.

Handling money and re-organizing my finances

were amongst the biggest practical problems I had after Jacques died. Most important, I had to change all my attitudes towards it – not to be frightened of money, to realize that I could handle it, and above all, to have enough confidence to believe I could make a decent living. Jacques, like many husbands, died intestate. This as it happened did not create any major problems for me, though it can prove disastrous for many widows. He also died with his financial affairs in something of a mess. Although not without assets and some insurance he had amassed considerable debts during the time of his illness which I was left to sort out. There was the question of whether I should sell the house or some of Jacques' paintings to pay off the debt. But I was in no state to make any major decision I might regret later on.

Many widows panic, including even those of rich, famous husbands. The novelist Graham Greene's widow, for example, initially believed she had been cut out of her husband's will, and sold some of the manuscripts of his early work. When the will was read, this proved unnecessary, as she had been well provided for.

Your first thought is 'How will I live?' It is certainly a shock if you find that your husband has left more debts than you ever knew about; and no widow, in those early frail first weeks, likes to think she will be forced to sell up. Finding out precisely where you stand financially is of vital importance. Many widows find that their financial position is not at all what they had imagined – suggesting, I suppose, that many men keep the real state of their financial affairs secret from their wives. It is extremely common for wives who have felt financially secure all their lives, to find on their husband's death that their liabilities far exceed their assets and that their husbands have in fact been under-insured, have run up credit card debts, overdrafts, and so on.

In my case, the mortgage on the house had automatically been paid off as part of the insurance; and it was only when a friend suggested that I look upon all my combined debts as a mortgage (which after all everybody had), and that I should in fact take out a small mortgage to cover that debt, and then not worry about it – that I started to lose my anxiety: it was, after all, a small amount compared to what many people owe on their homes. It was only, too, when I returned to work and gradually stepped up my writing that I began to have the confidence to realize that I could make a decent living if I worked hard enough, and that I would not be forced – at least not immediately – to sell anything. Having to make money in fact gave me the motivation to go on living and striving.

It took me all of two years to get the paperwork under control. My husband had not been particularly well organized, and in the beginning it was a job simply locating anything. Finding an old tax form could take weeks. I decided to re-file all the papers. I used the simple method of coloured files: yellow for bank, insurance and legal matters; blue for outstanding bills; pink for personal letters and so on. At the end of the week (usually on Friday afternoons when I had finished my newspaper column) I would go through the mass of correspondence and spend an hour or so just filing it. One of my friends told me the only way he could cope with the unwelcome task of catching up with bills was to sit down with a tumbler of whisky and then he could go through them all in quite a happy frame of mind! I had never been aware of the absolute *relentlessness* of bills, demands, legal enquiries and tax forms, all of which seem to need filling in in triplicate with information you never have to hand and have to rummage through three trunks or make six phone calls to locate. The piles of mail in the morning became a tyranny – and I used to dread the 'early morning thud' which meant another battle with forms, enquiries and bills. The brown envelopes of course are a daily reminder that you have taken on a new role as head of the household and sole provider. Sundays and Bank Holidays began to take on a new meaning – and I really began to look forward to them simply because there was no mail. The chaos that six months of illness and unemployment had brought to the household is reflected in this diary entry:

> Now I face the barrage of manilla envelopes each morning with an attempt at stoic calm. Make a strong cup of tea, brace myself, open them and at least make a gesture by putting them in piles. I'm reminded of the story of the artist John Bratby, who said he used to put all his bills in a suitcase and lock it in a wardrobe, hoping it would just go away. I am often tempted to do the same. It seems to help if you allow yourself a special time or day to tackle the whole ghastly process. The worst way to do it is to try and fit it between something more creative. This just doesn't work, and you end up thoroughly resenting all the paperwork for detracting you from your creativity (as if you didn't resent it

enough already). There is actually enormous satisfaction to be derived from polishing off a batch of bills. It is rather like appeasing the Gods.

Fortunately I had some help with this chaos in the shape of my lawyer, who was also an old family friend. In those first weeks, an early morning call from him was a life-saver. Not only would he make light of it all: 'Sod the bills,' he would say, 'Pay them all a little bit and keep them happy', good advice it turned out; but he would also entertain me with a stream of funny stories and one-liners. He was a natural comedian. I still remember laughing, in the midst of deepest gloom, at his stories of his yuppie clients with their 'offshore' companies, and how he would feel seasick if another client mentioned the word 'offshore'. I was amazed and almost shocked that I *could* laugh under such black conditions. It is comforting that our sense of the ridiculous can reassert itself anywhere: and there is no doubt that laughter *is* the best therapy. Anarchic humour enables you to say 'sod the world', even when perhaps you feel that your thoughts should be more sombre. Those early morning calls were the best possible medicine: they set me up for the day and helped me enormously in the first couple of years.

I gradually learned to adopt a more relaxed attitude towards money. My anxiety lessened as I realized I now, for the first time, had total (or as total as it could be) control over my finances – something I had never had in my marriage – and that there was a way of dealing with any financial crisis as long as I kept a cool head. I no longer felt I was drowning in a sea of manilla envelopes and for the first time in my life actually started to read the 'business and money' sections of the newspaper.

Learning how to handle my own money had again given me a new confidence. I would, however, recommend that all wives at some point spend a moment picturing themselves as a widow so that in terms of money alone they can prepare themselves and save themselves the terrible financial messes so many women find themselves in.

Chapter Five

A Death in the Family

'The family are seen as "too involved", too easily hurt by each other's grief. Also they may be in competition with each other to show a brave face or retain a position of respect.'

Colin Murray Parkes

A death affects not just individuals, but the whole family structure. The rebuilding of the family takes a long time. People have changed places. There have been re-alignments. Your daughter will never again be your daughter in the same way, just as your son will never quite be your son in the same way. These changes are subtle but nevertheless real. You may find one or another of your children trying to take the place of the dead person – suddenly perform his tasks and develop his interests; or perhaps just the opposite – return to the child's role and want you to take them on outings or get them treats just as you did when they were small.

I found my daughter had to go through a phase of taking on Jacques' identity, even re-enacting the last few months of his life (she became a carer for the terminally ill for a while), to identifying closely with me (she lived at home, travelled with me and helped me with some of my research), before slowly and painfully finding her own identity. The day she was able to take on a responsible challenging job and move into her own flat I knew the separation was complete and she had re-emerged as herself.

My son was 'stuck' for longer. He was not able to confront his father's death as openly as my daughter. His immediate reaction was to get himself 'engaged' to a fellow student and talk of imminent marriage. He obviously felt an immediate urge to form a new family. The relationship ended rather abruptly when reality set in, and both sides had second thoughts, and in spite of initial upset there was, I think, relief all round. Elias obviously had difficulty accepting change, wanting our home to be maintained exactly as it had been when he was a child. But gradually he has come round to accepting that my life and goals have changed and that he will not only have to think of his own life as an individual but allow me mine. He has even been instrumental in getting me to sort through and discard much of the junk we had collected over the years. But all this happened quite slowly and there have been periods of resistance when I have had patiently to allow him to come to terms with his feelings, instead of demanding that he change and move on. Patience is not my greatest virtue, yet it is one that is sorely needed when coping with children in this situation.

Many widows have told me that coping with their children's feelings – and grown-up children may be more difficult in some respects than very small ones – was more difficult for them than coping with their own. It is particularly difficult in the early months, since you are in a heightened state of anxiety *anyway* and you feel the awesome weight of being solely responsible for them. Teenage and grown-up children (ie in their early to late twenties) can react to bereavement in a variety of ways, depending on the degree of their attachment to the parent, the amount of expressed or unexpressed conflict, and the circumstances surrounding the death. I was particularly anxious because I knew that both my son and daughter had witnessed a gruesome death and that the wasted man they saw die was very far removed from the father they had known.

Both were singularly attached to their father, who had taken more than a usual part in their upbringing from birth. Being an older father and having lost his own family (he was forty when my son was born) he had been particularly indulgent towards them – seeing in them perhaps a chance to make amends for his lost childhood; and since he had always had his studio at home, he was able to spend far more time with them than the average father ever can. Mina, in her second year of college in Manchester, had insisted on coming home when she heard the news of Jacques' illness, temporarily abandoning her studies to help me nurse her father. This was not easy for a twenty-year-old girl, especially in the last weeks when there was such a terrible deterioration and she had to watch him virtually fade away before her very eyes. Elias was not able to confront the illness in quite the same way. At university in Wales, he distanced himself a little more – though, he too, towards the end, spent as much time as he was able with Jacques: and all three of us would help him, while he was still able, to take a short stroll each evening, as Jacques sang to the trees. Those walks were our last times together as a family, with Jacques fully conscious; and there was a terrible poignancy about them, as the children dutifully set off, propping him up on either side. Mina was there right until the end: Elias, although he said farewell to Jacques, had more trouble looking the ghastly illness straight in the eye.

Both children survived the funeral and Shiva well –

though Mina's severe depression started soon after. Elias seemed to remain ebullient, though he was far less open with his feelings and that, too, gave me some cause for concern. Above all I felt a terrible sadness for both children – knowing that Mina would not have a father to walk her up the aisle, and that Elias would not have Jacques there on graduation day (and how proud he would have been, since he himself deeply regretted not being able to complete his education because of the Nazis).

I often felt not quite up to the task of being everything to them. Like any single parent, there were moments when their moods and problems completely wore me out and I longed for some escape. Just as the new mother needs mothering, the newly widowed does too, and the strain of being a twenty-four-hour mother can prove unbearable in the beginning. It is important, I think, to acknowledge any resentment and from time to time let go and have a good screaming or shouting session.

> I know that my poor children occasionally have to bear the brunt of my outbursts. This often happens when they come to spend a day or two at home. I don't like myself for doing it, but like all people who live alone, I store up feelings of anger, and it takes the most flimsy of straws to break the camel's back. I would often surprise myself with the violence of my outbursts – occasioned very often by only some minor thoughtlessness. On one occasion it was one of the children cleaning out the fridge and eating the meal I had prepared for the following day. Why

didn't they realize that I had cooked two days' meals in advance because it is more convenient for me? Answer – because they still remember the old days when the fridge was bursting with food, when I would cook for armies and the house was like a virtual hotel. These days I have to plan food very carefully. I no longer keep open house, I no longer service people's needs in the same way and I think that some of my resentment springs from the children's non-recognition both of my new role, and how far I have come. I have moved on and they expect me to be the old-style mum. It is so hard for them: I weep for them, seeing me so vulnerable.

To their credit both children in fact have survived even the worst of my moods pretty well, with our roles being well and truly reversed at times. 'Call me anytime, Mum,' my daughter would say, reminding me that she was as capable of being my support at times, as I was hers. While Elias, where he could, would try to offer me advice about work, relationships, the house and garden. I think it is important to allow one's children at times to assume the caring role, though of course, as their parent, remaining very aware that essentially you must be there for them. The role reversal can only be occasional, and is part of the changing dynamic of the family.

Families seem to react to a widow in their midst in one of two ways: either they are tremendously supportive and loving or else they almost seem to turn their backs on her until 'normality' returns (when she has met another man, or 'accepted' her lot as a widow, possibly years later). I know that certain relatives only seemed able to relate to me normally when I showed them I was really OK, when I assured them I was dating again, enjoying my work and was optimistic about the future: in other words, I no longer had 'the taint of death' about me. Many families do not want to know the grieving widow: her grief remains unacknowledged and their seeming indifference or callousness can appear wounding again and again, as I know from my own experience.

It is a complaint I hear so often from the bereaved: 'I thought my own family would be marvellous – but they haven't in fact, been very supportive at all.' I now know that only exceptionally strong people can confront someone else's despair head-on, and that perhaps one's own family, where unresolved rivalries and old resentments are bound to exist, are not the best people to do so. Because my own mother almost simultaneously was a widow too, I tried to spare her feelings and would attempt to hide my grief from her. I often found myself 'playing' the strong woman, the coping member of the family since there seemed no one capable of doing so. Two of my brothers lived abroad at that time and most of my aunts and uncles were ageing with problems of their own: again I felt obliged to spare them.

There were only two family members (outside of my own children) to whom I communicated the full extent of my grief: one was a second cousin who needed no prompting to call and visit, the other an elderly recently widowed aunt, who, like me, felt similarly isolated. I would make a point of phoning her every weekend to exchange experiences and feelings – and although we had never been particularly close before we found we could both open up to one another without the fear of exacerbating or compounding each other's bad feelings.

I would urge anyone who is feeling a sense of being let down by close family members to look a little further, to someone perhaps on the fringes of the family who is better able to handle troubled emotions. Above all you don't want to have to worry about the other person's reactions: it is simply acceptance you are after.

Other people's attitudes towards the mourner or the bereaved can best be explained in terms of their own anxiety about loss and abandonment. My own experience bears this out: people whom I might have expected to be very supportive and helpful at the time often tended to stay away in the months following the death, including certain members of my own family; but we forget the ripples a death can cause in other people's lives which perhaps explains the avoidance behaviour. This can apply to those whose marriage is going through a particularly rocky patch: one loss forces them to think of the possibility of another. The death of a spouse can start a sort of chain-reaction on their perception of their own marriage and indeed force them to rethink their whole lives. Their marriage may have been in trouble for years, but death merely focuses their attention on their own crisis. Or one of the partners may have uneasy relationships with other close family members and the death merely serves to remind them that one day they too might experience a loss before all the 'unfinished business' has been done.

The newly bereaved are exceptionally sensitive to what appear to them to be other people's slights. In the first year I was mightily aggrieved – hurt and disappointed – by the people who had not felt able or bothered to phone, write or keep in contact with me:

every widow knows those who will even cross the street to avoid talking to them. Mostly it is a reflection of their own very great discomfort with loss suffering – but you do not immediately perceive it as such.

I remember feeling terribly hurt because some individuals made it very clear to me that I was now considered a potential drain on their time: someone who might ask to be met at a station, or have her lawn mown. One or two made it very clear that I was now to be avoided in case I expected 'special favours' from their husbands. In fact, no such favours were sought, but the husbands were not allowed to see me or talk to me on my own just in case I would make demands of some kind. This had the effect of not only making me feel deeply disappointed in these individuals, but of making me more fiercely independent (at least on the surface) than I actually was. Bravado made me 'invent' friends who were helping me, advisers who didn't exist – and all because I felt too deeply hurt to show them my intense vulnerability. Many widows do this: they affect an enormous front of coping rather than own up to feelings of extreme helplessness and despair. It was only when I found the courage to reveal the true extent of my hurt and dependency that I actually became emotionally more independent from the people I felt had failed me.

I found that some people remained curiously silent after Jacques' death – who, during his lifetime, had claimed to be friends. One, on finally being contacted, made the excuse that they had had no personal reply to a condolence letter; others claimed they had lost my number. What they were doing was simply finding the first excuse to discontinue the relationship, which had really been with Jacques. Many widows find this: that close friends of their husband drop them because there were few ties or little feeling to begin with. It is deeply upsetting at a time when you are already extremely vulnerable and feeling like a social pariah; but as time passes, you may even feel a sense of relief at losing some of these people with whom, in reality, you had very little in common.

I have lost perhaps thirty percent of my friends and acquaintances who had only valued me as Jacques' wife and saw no reason to maintain a relationship with me as an individual. Mourning completes all relationships – not only your own with the person you have lost – but other people's with you. It is a subtle shake-up of the kaleidoscope – some shapes will inevitably disappear. The friends you make after bereavement are very special. They are part of your new identity. They have never known you as part of a couple. They will value you not as a part of a couple, but for who you are.

Many widows experience a sense of being a social outcast. Some will even exacerbate the process and find some small pretext to pick quarrels with everyone in the family or close circle. It is almost like a child saying, 'I'm unloveable anyway – so why don't I make myself more so, just to see who will still love me?' It is a way of testing relationships (sometimes to the limit). It is not uncommon for the bereaved to go into a self-induced limbo. It is due, I am convinced, to the feelings of low self-esteem and worthlessness which make the person experiencing the loss challenge others to *prove* their worth. This is a mixture of defensiveness and childish regression on the part of the mourner and other people working out and expressing more negative aspects of their own relationship with you. It is not unknown for the bereaved to quarrel with every single one of their relatives and close acquaintances in the months directly following their loss. It is partly because of all the old hurts that surface and partly because of a changing family dynamic where there may be some real power shifts, especially with the death of the senior males. Susan Hill describes this beautifully in her poignant *In the Springtime of the Year*, the semi-autobiographical novel about the way a young widow comes to terms with her anger and grief, and finally finds comfort in a relationship with a young boy.

You will not grow a tough outer skin for some time: the hurts will keep coming, which does not necessarily mean you will become embittered. Death affects different personalities differently. It has a different meaning to everyone. Just as you bring everything you are to giving birth, so too you bring everything you are to death. The bitter, resentful personality will be even more embittered by bereavement, an envious one even more envious of other lives left intact, untouched by tragedy; a self-pitying person will become even more so. Those who felt their lives lacking in meaning before the loss will only have this meaninglessness confirmed. Death, in other words, confirms all our negative feelings about both ourselves and the world. Intertwined with this is the feeling 'I deserved this to happen. I deserve to be alone.' It is tempting to think in one's lower moments: 'I have been badly treated because I am bad.' It is this sense of worthlessness that leads so many widows to almost suicidal depression. A wonderful little book called *When Bad Things Happen to Good People* by Harold Kushner answers all the 'Why Me?' questions people who experience tragedies are apt to torment themselves with. When this feeling does strike it is as well to remind yourself that no one deserves bad things to happen to them.

Chapter Six

A Special Place

'For life and death are one. Even as the river and sea are one.'

Kahlil Gibran, *The Prophet*

I have always found visiting Jacques' grave a great comfort. The graveyard was situated about three miles from my home in a pleasant parkland setting. In the beginning I would go frequently – nearly every week, choosing days preferably when the sun shone and I was not feeling too low. Later on I didn't feel the same need to go as frequently and my visits either corresponded with an anniversary, a momentous event or a sudden urge to go and express certain feelings. These two journal entries were both written in the first year:

> I usually go when I find I am really stuck with a problem for which there looks like being no solution. I go to ask Jacques for guidance – somehow to show me a way through. Without giving a supernatural explanation, what may happen is that you focus your energies hard – and allow for an answer to come through. You open yourself up, so to speak.
>
> I always leave flowers (though not a very Jewish custom) because it's my way of giving something. Why shouldn't one have a relation-

ship, or extend one's relationship with the dead? I will after all never really stop having a relationship with the man who was the father of my children and to whom I was married for close on a quarter of a century.

The air is crisp and cold after an unseasonably mild spell and the skies bright blue. My spirits are lifted after shopping in the High Street and feeling invigorated by the good weather. I want to visit Jacques' grave – today I can face it: the hour has come to speak to my darling; to tell him I am doing all right; that I struggle through two to three hours of paperwork every day; that I have settled the children; that I phone builders and banks, lawyers, tax officials, that I pay bills, empty dustbins, that each day I grow a little stronger – no less lonely – but a little stronger; that I no longer feel when I walk down a street that the sign 'widow' is pinned to me; that I managed to go up to London this week, and take the train back again to the big empty house where he used to wait for me; that his love still sustains me. I dress in my best tartan skirt, black sweater and favourite coat that he bought for me for my last birthday. It is strange how I still wear the clothes he loved to visit the grave – but it feels right and shows I still have a sense of his guiding presence.

I go down to the market and buy three bunches of sweet-smelling jonquils. (I know he will like these as a sign of spring) and then I get a taxi to the cemetery. The taxi driver says nothing: he knows my sorrow. I ask him to wait and walk down the path where I walked unsightedly on the day of the funeral. I take in the pretty rolling hills and trees, and think that Jacques must be at peace here. I lay my flowers on the earth at the grave and tell Jacques everything I wanted to. Then I return to the waiting taxi, and I know Jacques has heard and I feel at peace.

Sometimes my mood is sad and self-doubting. All the old guilts re-emerge. In the cemetery I allow myself to feel the guilt for the past. Death allows one to see so clearly that which was a miasma then. But I realize it is useless to have regrets about my own ability to comprehend totally at the time, and my own concern with the mundane, the practical and the domestic which at times I know oppressed him, and yet which he needed too. Our partnership, I see now, had been, as all relationships, a strange and precarious balance, which at times my own fragility tipped too much one way or the other. I think back to the years when I was ill, and yet I am the one who is still here and he is gone.

The Sri Lankan taxi driver who has been waiting for me brings me back to earth as he muses in pidgin English about life and death. I am always struck by the differences between the cab drivers who take me to the cemetery: the English ones often say nothing afterwards – driving me home in silence; or start to whistle or change the subject entirely. I am aware of their intense embarrassment. I find myself apologizing for keeping them waiting. Some ask me who it is I am visiting.

Others say nothing. The Indian and Pakistani drivers, on the other hand, want to talk about death. They ask me how Jacques died; how long I have been a widow, and inevitably start to philosophize: 'Why is there this cancer?' asked one. Why indeed? I almost felt sorry for his incomprehension – I tried to enlighten him . . . Once again I find myself trying to ease someone else's discomfort. My thoughts too on that occasion turned to the illness itself – the cemetery being the place where I allow myself to think about the unthinkable. But there are positive feelings too. It is natural to want to renew life, which is why the carefully tended plots with their miniature gardens mean so much. The instinct is very great in me too.

A year later I decided that I wanted some continual signs of life by Jacques' grave, something cheerful to look at in spring; so I bought a huge bag of daffodil bulbs and summoned up the energy one October day to go there to plant them.

A blue and gold autumn day and at last I had enough energy and courage to plant a hundred daffodils I had been storing in the summerhouse. My neighbour, George, lent me a tool, a 'dibber', to dig the holes with. The ground was muddy and it worked like a charm. The act of planting all those bulbs gave me a sense of accomplishment. I concentrated intensely – pushing two or three bulbs into each hole. Wet loose turf was everywhere. I flattened it down and pictured a small patch of waving daffodils and narcissi in the spring, softening the harsh gravestone. Jacques would have loved it – and I think of coming generations who will see the daffodils. There is a comfort in this vision of the future. There is a sense of rounding something off – as if I am completing some special task.

I talk to the oak tree nearby. It is huge and gnarled, and changes with the seasons. I always focus on it when I visit the cemetery. Sometimes it 'becomes' Jacques; and at other times it suggests his enduring presence. Above all it is an anchor for my thoughts. Just above the oak, I have a place I see in my mind where his presence, spirit, call it what you wish, hovers. Every time I go to place my flowers on the grave, I look above the tree into the sky and I know that he is there.

Everyone needs a special place where they feel they can sense the presence of the person they have lost. I am something of a pantheist (how easy it is to understand those beliefs). I have a special spot in the garden (a luxuriant border of marguerites) where I feel I can communicate with God personally. It is so important after a tragedy or loss of any kind to be able to pray and communicate with God – yet so many people find it impossible. A friend of mine who had had her flat burnt to the ground told me that she had been desperate to pray – to thank God for sparing her life from the fire; and to that end she had gone to a synagogue one Friday evening. There she found much to her dismay she could not pray at all. Simply nothing came. She went to her favourite clearing in a wood, however, and found she could open her heart. We all need our own 'sacred' spot: this is why I don't regard visiting the grave as something morbid. On the contrary it can bring great relief.

Six months later I attend the funeral of an old man in the Jewish community and write:

> The Jewish part of the cemetery is so small that one can count the newly dug graves and headstones one by one, and remember each as a friend: a true 'community of the dead'. For one moment during the most solemn part of the ceremony – the lowering of the coffin and the shovelling of the earth – my heart lifts a little. Why? I can glimpse the daffodil bulbs I planted, a full six inches of growth, dotting Jacques' grave. The big oak tree – his tree – is bare now – but the flowers will bloom again – and I feel a surge of renewal which is the very opposite of bleak.

I was to visit the cemetery many times in the first year or two, and I never felt ashamed of my need to do so. The trees and flowers were to assume many meanings to me until I was able one day simply to visualize my oak.

Almost two and a half years after Jacques died I wrote:

> The day before my birthday: always a lonely time – although everyone around me has made a huge effort to make the day a good

one. Today I feel the need to visit the
cemetery and plant the two bush roses I
bought last week – one red, one yellow – to
remind me of the six dozen red and yellow
roses Jacques brought me on one of our first
dates in New York in 1964, making me feel
like an operatic Diva on her first night.

I have come just in time to see the
wonderful array of daffodils and narcissi
dancing around the grave in the cold March
wind. The sight of them fills me with – if not
exactly joy – a feeling of 'rightness' about the
world. Spring is still here. Jacques would
have been happy. Once he would have
picked spring flowers, arranged them in one
of his favourite vases, taken it up to the studio
and painted it. I was forever scolding him for
taking all my best flower arrangements. Now
only daffodils dance on his grave. My special
oak tree is just coming into bloom. Once
again I tell it all about my new activities as
well as the children's news. Surrounded by
primroses and daffodils, I almost have a
feeling of exuberance. It has been important
for me to remember those red and yellow
roses: Jacques' love of nature and above all
colour had helped rid him of some of the
sadness of his Holocaust past.

I think as I walk through the cemetery that
I too still feel that sadness on his behalf from
time to time. Only now perhaps I am
beginning to understand why he chose to
absorb himself in nature and painting: how
he came through his art to make sense of the

chaotic and nightmarish memories.

July 1991:

> I no longer feel the same urge to visit the
> grave, except on anniversaries and special
> days. I seem to have integrated any thinking
> about Jacques more into my everyday thoughts
> and conversation. It is not so much I no
> longer think about him or wish to communi-
> cate with him, but that I now take it for
> granted – that it is part of my life and
> consciousness.

Winter 1992:

> I am happy now to think of the daffodils that
> will come every spring. I can picture them in
> my mind without actually being there,
> though there are days when I still get the
> urge to physically stand in the spot, and gaze
> up at that tree. Now it is usually to announce
> something happy or momentous in my life.
> Living has taken over.

Chapter Seven

The Widow Kupfermann

'For she must not simply sit and sit, as though the blood was dammed up within her.'

Susan Hill, *In the Springtime of the Year*

The widow in the first few months after bereavement finds herself having to cope not only with disturbed sleep patterns, low energy reserves, depression, confusion and anxiety over money matters; she is also confronted, above all, by the loneliness of silence. Many widows tell of their distress at sitting in an empty, silent room, night after night, or as they sit alone watching television, or waiting for the phone to ring.

A journal entry written in the first year after Jacques died reminds me how difficult I found this silence to cope with:

> Widowhood has definitely made me more chatty and outgoing in one sense. I'm forced to be – otherwise there would be unbearably long hours of silence and isolation. You don't know how long a day can seem until forced to be entirely in your own company. I notice now that I witter on to everybody – taxi drivers, hairdresser, people in supermarket queues, banks, on trains and buses – you have to find a 'sounding board' everywhere, for home can feel so lonely now that there is

no one to talk to. You forget the continual buzz of chat, the continual dialogue, even if it is punctuated by silences, that goes on between husband and wife: all those remarks, all those exchanges – about everything from putting out the cat to the meaning of life; and when that is gone, how you can feel as if you're in solitary confinement.

It is very important to strike up conversations with whoever is available, to reach out, through phone calls, letters, chance encounters and so on. Normally quite a reserved person, I am sure people consider me much more garrulous these days as I am always eager to talk. Talking is my greatest luxury. It may be ruinous on the phone bill, but it salvages my sanity. The other bonus is that forcing yourself to talk to everyone – from shopkeepers to bus conductors – makes you a more 'local' person. It is quite amazing the information you pick up casually about local life. Often, in a marriage, you forget how you operate as a virtually self-contained unit since all your needs are met at home. As a single person this simply isn't possible, which necessitates an enormous re-adjustment.

Breaking the loneliness barrier necessitates an awareness of just how isolated and dependent you have been in the married state. Married couples very often are 'islands' unto themselves: they have constructed their social reality together which may exclude many people they were never aware of excluding. I had never before, for example, developed much of a relationship with my neighbours – that is, as individuals. We had known them as a couple, talking to them occasionally over the fence, in the driveway, or once a year over the statutory Boxing Day drink. But with the emergencies of both my father's death and Jacques' illness, I had been forced to call upon them for the practical help with driving and shopping they had so kindly volunteered, and through that had built up a new, deeper friendship with them. I now looked forward to dropping in once or twice a week for tea or coffee. They had seen me at my very lowest ebb: I could relax and be myself with them. Having a cup of tea did not make the same demands as a dinner party. I would allow myself time each day to call on one or other of the neighbours: this would break up the day, and provide the chat I so longed for. Eventually these forays became more ambitious – though I still retained a very strong sense of wanting to remain cocooned. Neighbours were safe: other people, the world out there, was still a threat.

So strong were my feelings of wanting to remain cocooned that in the early months I virtually had to force myself to go out in the evenings. Not surprisingly, my early attempts at socializing were often less than successful and left me feeling bruised and battered. I had reckoned neither on my own hypersensitivity and changing reactions to people nor on friends' reactions to me. For a while I was quite paranoid about my status. I worried about casting a pall on the occasion – and sensed people either retreating as I entered a room, or adopting a mask of forced cheerfulness. The only area where I felt even half-way confident was with other writers, though even there I could come a cropper. I well remember a feminist lunch I attended soon after Jacques died, where a group of high-powered feminist authors went into a predictable diatribe against men. I ended up feeling physically sick, especially since I knew that most of them had husbands who were helping to support them. That was a particularly misjudged outing. If I had thought about the women invited, I might have realized that the main topic of conversation would be how much they hated men. But at this stage, having just lost the man in my life, this was not exactly what I wanted to hear. At any other time I might have enjoyed the bitchiness and banter.

Many bereaved people feel that their grief is not sufficiently acknowledged, that others want to avoid the subject, which is something I too was to experience very soon after my loss. I remember being invited about three months or so after Jacques' death to a dinner party by friends I considered fairly close. There were two other couples there: one, complete strangers to me, but the other, an editor and his artist wife, had known us both quite well. I was therefore taken aback when he asked me brightly, 'So what have you been up to lately? I haven't seen your column.' I quickly realized that my hosts had told him nothing about what had happened and I felt angry, shocked, and hugely embarrassed at having to divulge at that very moment at a social gathering, in front of strangers, the details of Jacques' death and of my own circumstances. Even more surprising and shocking was the reaction of all present. A total silence fell over the table for about two minutes, and then the conversation simply switched abruptly to the publication of someone's latest book, and everyone got on with their meal as if nothing had happened. I never heard from any of the people present again. I felt rather as if I had announced that I had contracted some 'social disease'. This sort of reaction not only treats death as a taboo subject but is cruelly indifferent to the feeling of the bereaved person who wants – not sympathy – but at least an acknowledgement of some change in her status. How much, after all, would it have taken to have briefly clued the other guests in beforehand? I now know that if I am introducing the recently bereaved at a social gathering I let the other guests know something of their circumstances so that they are not going to put them in a similarly embarrassing position at having to reveal all when perhaps they are feeling at their most vulnerable and insecure.

In the early days I seemed to have absolutely no judgement as to the kind of social events that would benefit me; on the contrary, I seemed to be almost irresistibly drawn towards events guaranteed to make me feel the most pain. Or perhaps, looking at it another way, it could have been that it had not yet registered with people that my situation had changed and so they went on inviting me to the kind of events I would have happily attended with Jacques. (Of course, if they hadn't invited me, I would have been upset too!) There was for example, the silver wedding reception at a very fancy club that had me in paroxysms of misery for days afterwards. It was a very splendid affair, and I had assumed that there would be at least a couple of single people there. I had assumed wrong, for looking around at the various tables I recognized couple after couple that I knew, but not one person on their own. True, I was seated with old friends who spent most of the time telling me how good it was for me to go out – but the very fact that I had known them all a long time seemed to aggravate my sadness; for it occurred to me that every single one of them would shortly be celebrating their silver wedding, and I was seized with a desolate feeling of 'Why am I the only one not to be celebrating?' What had any of them done to deserve this?

Other widows will be familiar with these feelings, ignoble but understandable, of bitterness and envy which strike at times: the sense of 'Why me?' when the whole world seems to be composed of smug and fortunate couples and you feel rather like a tree that has been cut down in full bloom. I had never had these strong feelings of envy before and it came as something of a shock to realize I was wallowing in self-pity. The only reasonable thing to do is to stay away from 'couples only' situations that will bring out these feelings – that is, until you are strong enough to cope with them, when a greater sense of proportion has set in and you can even (as I do now, four years on) see some benefits in the single state. But it has to be said that in the early days it hurts like hell, and I will never forget the agony of sitting through speech after speech at that evening, extolling a long and happy marriage, and then watching like some wistful wallflower as the couples got up one by one to dance. At that stage I couldn't see that many of them were not exactly enjoying 'love-affairs' and may even have been envying me my single state. All I could feel was desolation and the sense of having been deprived.

That other widows also feel this resentment against couples is seen in this extract from a letter I received, from a forty-two-year-old widow called Kathleen:

> The rage and jealousy I have had against other women who still have their husbands and their damned pretty life has only begun to calm down recently. I saw a therapist

several times a week – still see her once a
fortnight or so. That helped me cope more
than anything, even my friends. They were
supportive but I was always aware that they
had their own lives to attend to, that one of
these days I would see their eyes glaze over,
and know that they had had enough. That
the next time I saw them, I would have to
force myself to be someone else, to be happy,
to talk about other things, so they would not
think, 'Oh there she goes'. So that they would
want to see me again. I lost several friends
because I was so hurt at how unsupportive
they were – women and men. If I met
someone through a friend, and they had been
told I was a widow, they immediately had
this frozen smile on their faces, as if they were
thinking 'How soon? What shape is she in?' It
made me sick.

All widows worry that if they turn down invitations
in the early days, they will simply stop receiving any. I
have heard this expressed a hundred times. 'In the
beginning I was invited all the time, and I didn't feel
like going, now no one invites me anymore,' is the *cri
de coeur* of every widow (though not, it must be said, of
every widower, since they are always at a social
premium, and considered a great catch for a dinner
table). It is extremely difficult to get the balance right –
especially in the early weeks when people tend to
invite you out of a sense of duty or of misplaced
kindness, when possibly you'd rather they came over
and spent some time with you in your own home,
where you feel safe and don't have to make the effort of

dinner-party conversation or of getting dressed up. If I were to be cynical, I could say that people's compassion does not last long. I was very aware of certain token gestures made in the early days ('Oh, we'll invite poor old Jeannette') which did not extend further than the first six months. After this I was no longer thought of in these terms, but definitely as more of a threat. I noticed the invitations to dinner with my married friends became fewer and I was relegated to the position of unfortunate maiden aunt.

Sometimes it was like a black comedy: for example I remember the time I was invited as an afterthought to lunch with two octogenarians to help get rid of leftovers from the big event (couples only, of course) the night before. On another occasion I was invited to tea by a very well-meaning older couple; and as I walked into the room and was introduced I noticed not one or even two single women, but six elderly ladies, all of whom it seems were widows of some standing. It was rather like walking into some Victorian sewing circle, and my first impulse was to giggle. Here was I, the 'novice' widow, being introduced to the 'old hands'. I felt rather like Scarlett O'Hara, and suddenly, quite wickedly, had the desire to shock, or do something outrageous. What is the collective noun for widows? A gaggle? Whatever it was, I had just walked into it.

I think it was at that precise moment that I first became aware that I had a new label – 'the Widow Kupfermann' as a friend teasingly calls me. Widow is an ugly word, deriving from the Sanskrit for 'empty'. I have heard many others say they could not bring themselves to use the word 'widow' and for a long time I could not actually say the word. If anyone asked

me about my marital status, I would hum and hah –
and obliquely refer to my 'late' husband; but I simply
could not get myself to say point-blank, 'I am a widow'.
Widows were other people; they were not me; they
were all those sallow-faced Mediterraneans dressed
permanently in black with ferociously blazing eyes –
the sort of widow the Greek actress Irene Papas
immortalized on screen. Alternatively they had blue
rinses, wore flashy diamond rings, took cruises round
the world and gambled. They lived in hotels in
Eastbourne, and I was always running into them on
trains travelling to see their daughters in Plymouth or
Aberdeen. Most widows I'd ever met seemed to be
permanently on the move – shuffled around from
relative to relative – a sort of forgotten regiment of
women in transit.

I was of course still perceiving the widow as others
saw her, and I had not until then identified with any of
the stereotypes. Now here was I, the 'young widow',
being introduced as a new member of a club, and my
instinct was to run. I've heard others say this, and not
just widows or the bereaved: I know for instance of
people with mild forms of multiple sclerosis who were
persuaded to attend an MS meeting, and who – on
finding there others similarly or more severely
afflicted – have felt a great deal worse about their
predicament.

I suppose this is because we have not yet fully
accepted what has happened. We are still denying it.
There is a great life-force within us all, whatever
tragedy or disaster we have endured, that makes us
crave normality – even fun and distraction – at the
worst of times. What I most wanted at that moment
was a light-hearted lunch with a mixed bunch of

people, rather than commiserating with others in a similar plight.

It took me a long while before I stopped bursting into tears every time I told someone I was a widow: the emotions are so near the surface, that the smallest conceived slight or even unintentional insensitivity on somebody's part can wound. It's hardly any wonder; you have little sense of self. The social reality that you spent so many years carefully constructing with your partner has been demolished. Your world has fallen apart, you don't know where to begin, and everyone seems to be pressuring you to get going – to build up a new reality and identity – to resume your old identity, to fill in the social hole. You can only of course build up this new identity step by step. This encompasses new friends (terribly important – for the old are still seeing you in your old role, whereas new friends make you feel you have an identity of your own – that you are worth knowing as a person as well as just half a couple).

I would hold that these new friends (plus financial security) are the most important step to making a recovery. They may come from completely unexpected quarters; they may be completely different types from those you knew with your partner – for you are a different person. You may be surprised at your own tastes, for so many women have had to accept their husband's friends, many of whom may have been business acquaintances. Indeed many wives may never have had the opportunity to choose their friends during their marriage. Now things are different; you have complete freedom of choice – and this very freedom of course can present a problem and be quite dizzying.

I found myself reaching out for friendship in the most unexpected places – whether it was on a Greek island, teaming up with a couple of teenagers, or talking to strangers on trains. Many discover as I did that it can be much easier to reveal one's feelings to complete strangers who have never known the old you. It is not always a rewarding experience – sometimes it became a frightening and desolate exercise and you have to make very sure that the person on the receiving end actually wants to receive your confidences and see you revealed in all your vulnerability. All widows have to resist the temptation to unburden themselves to all and sundry. Not everyone is willing to hear what you have to say, and there were occasions where I became aware that I was unloading an unfair burden on to someone. It's important to judge your audience; though it is surprising just how many people do want to hear and will lend a ready ear.

In my case, after a flurry in the first few months, the invitations stopped; and for a while I felt I had disappeared altogether off the social scene. Then I started to appreciate just how difficult it was for other people to gauge my state of mind and how far I had progressed in my mourning. I realized I would have to take the initiative. This was very difficult as there is nothing one feels less like doing in those early days of depression, lack of confidence and energy, than picking up a phone and saying, 'Can I come over?' or 'Why don't we go here, there, or wherever?' For a while I virtually stopped going anywhere until, slowly, the desire to see or do something, anything, overtook me. It was partly the realization that I was becoming horribly dull – and as a writer I needed outside stimuli. This awareness in itself was a healthy thing, for it meant that I was thinking about survival and that part of me, in spite of the numbness, depression and apathy, was functioning – the professional part of me that says, however low you are feeling, you have to force yourself to do certain things just because you have to eat.

Commitment to life starts with very small things: summoning the energy to re-activate your old network is one of them. This is especially important after bereavement, when you often feel you are cut off from the rest of the world: when even making a phone call to a long-established friend seems onerous and daunting. It is too easy to let your contacts drop – to let one day slide into another – never making the call or writing the letter which could make all the difference. I am a great believer, in spite of everything I have gone through, that one creates one's own good luck. My advice, therefore is to wait for the mood to strike you (there is no point in forcing it) and on a good day make as many calls as you can in a concentrated period. You will be amazed at your own daring – and having once plucked up the courage, this will give you the confidence to do it again – and confidence is precisely what suffers most with bereavement. As Melanie Klein wrote in 'Mourning and its Relationship to Manic-Depressive States' (*International Journal of Psycho-Analysis*, 21, 125): 'The pain experienced in the slow process of testing reality in the work of mourning seems to be partly due to the necessity, not only to renew the links to the external world, and thus continuously re-experience the loss, but at the same time, and by means of this, to rebuild with anguish the inner world which is felt to be in danger of deteriorating and collapsing.'

I found it very difficult to get the balance right; in fact, to be honest, there was no balance in my life at this moment. Some weeks I would force myself to see four films in succession followed by three exhibitions and a concert. Others I would stay at home every evening, and spend my time immersed in trashy novels. My life was progressing in fits and starts. I wanted somebody to help me, but I knew the help had to come from me.

Entertaining is a very important way of maintaining social ties, yet it is here widows can feel most at a loss and so many tell me they have no social life because they can no longer entertain. There *are* ways of providing hospitality however that cause minimal strain. It is obviously very difficult entertaining single-handed, but one of my greatest joys is having the house full of people at weekends – dinner parties may be cumbersome and out of the question – but there is nothing wrong with having people for tea. I sometimes still feel the echoes of all the past teas; it was a pattern initiated by my father, his favourite being Saturday tea in the garden (however inclement the weather).

When Jacques had been alive we had served high summer teas under the pear tree on a white wrought-iron table; I had always used the pretty delphinium blue and white china Jacques had bought me as a present from Biba's in its heyday – and had liked to serve tiny egg and tomato sandwiches, lots of watercress, chocolate and apple cake followed by mounds of strawberries or cherries. Jacques would often be painting in another part of the garden and had to secure his canvas with rocks or something similar before joining us. Tea in the garden had even been extended to Fuchsia Cottage in Cornwall, where we would drag out the kitchen table on to our little front patio surrounded by the large fuchsia bushes, and entertain our friends to tea and saffron cake – and occasionally mackerel suppers when Jacques would clean, gut and fry the freshly caught fish himself.

I realize I will never recreate those days but I still get joy from the same blue and white china and these days tea is likely to be served in my newly created patio area, on the small marble-topped ice cream parlour table, and be for three or four people only. Entertaining people at home is a way of showing to the world that you have created some order in your life again. It is a way of proving it to yourself, too. One sunny July afternoon in 1988 when I had people wandering casually through my house again looking at paintings and the garden filled with talk and laughter I knew my world was on the way to being re-built.

As I gradually 'uncoupled' and discovered my own identity and wholeness, I learned to feel less threatened by a world which did, at one point, seem to be geared entirely towards couples. I no longer hankered after invitations to dinner parties, much preferring to have lunch with a single individual or group of people I liked for their individual qualities. I learned to enjoy spontaneity and simply have fun – but it did not happen overnight.

As I became more of an individual I also found myself assuming new roles. One of them was the role of 'comforter' – which, as a mourner yourself, you slip into very easily, though at times you may feel, as I did, reluctant to play the part, as it usually means a painful reminder of all the grief of those early days. More often, however, I felt a kind of pride in my new role, as this extract from my journal shows:

> Another neighbour has died on the Terrace
> leaving a widow in her fifties – an extremely
> pleasant cheerful woman who volunteered
> her help again and again when Jacques was in
> hospital. I seem to be called upon to comfort
> mourners more and more often. In the
> beginning I found it difficult: I had little
> comfort to give. Now I almost feel that I have
> grown into a role of professional mourner and
> comforter – that indeed I have a special
> qualification for the role. I feel part of a band
> of women – a group of 'wise women' if you
> wish – whose baptism and initiation through
> fire has given them a special role to play as
> collaborator, sympathizer with them in their
> suffering. It does not depress me. On the
> contrary, it gives my life a new meaning. I
> have entered the ranks of the wise.

Chapter Eight

Expectations and Stereotypes

'The power of the family will inevitably be used to try and force the grieving person into line if he or she fails to meet their expectations.'

Dr Tony Lake

You know that you have come a long way when you no longer react to other people's discomfiture at death. The first year or so for me was a nightmare of prickly paranoia. My expectation of how I thought people *should* behave or how I desperately wanted them to behave, so rarely corresponded with the reality. There are several possible explanations for this. Either the *needs* of the recently bereaved are so great that they literally scare people away and force them to behave in quite the contrary fashion – which is something Lily Pincus believes: 'Nobody wants feelings of panic and despair recalled, and hence they neglect them in the mourner, which in time confirms his worst fears – that he is isolated without love and comfort' (from *Death in the Family*). Or alternatively it is a question of balance of power, other people being aware of your relative powerlessness and exerting all *their* power to force you to meet *their* expectations. One sees this in hundreds of different things, from the way close family and friends will urge a woman to move house immediately, return to work, pull herself together, or go out more. Unthreatening normality is *their* world before loss: and one which they urge you to return to.

At times I felt pressured to recover from my

mourning as quickly as possible. This seemed to be what people wanted, hence their insistent questions: 'Are you back at work yet? Are you getting out?' and their admiring comments when I appeared to be 'brave' (how I loathe that word). 'Isn't she marvellous!' I didn't feel marvellous – only convinced that people wanted me back to normal as soon as possible.

I particularly resented those who told me how I ought to be feeling: the stage I ought to be at. Some spoke to me like a text-book. 'By now you should have exorcized your guilt and anger and be on to the next stage.' Someone even asked: 'Are you crying enough?' I cried when I heard this. What was this? An examination one had to pass? Was there a correct and incorrect way to mourn? What if I got it wrong? This fear became an additional burden. I had the same feeling experienced by many widows that I was expected to 'grieve' between seven and ten on Saturdays – somewhere else – that my grief was marginalized – that I wasn't being allowed to 'be' in my grief.

It wasn't until about two years after Jacques' death that I could write in my diary:

> One thing I've realized over these two years or so is that as a widow one has at all costs to resist other people's expectations of your behaviour. Other people will try to mould you, make you try to conform in some way to their wishes – where you should live (I was amazed when certain people even described in architectural detail and design the sort of house or rather flat I should remove myself to as soon as possible). They will even suggest

wallpaper to you. It may not go as far as garden gnomes *but* they will suggest perhaps concreting over your front lawn. Some will try to persuade you to move closer to your children, or the exact opposite. Family and friends will persuade you to invest your money in a certain way, or even stock up your freezer with certain items. Your hairstyle, wardrobe, diet, leisure activities, holidays, work patterns, all become subject to a new scrutiny. Remaining single and reasonably happy is particularly deplored. It is unnatural, one of my friends insisted – even though it was quite clear I was managing very well and was enjoying a freedom I had never had before.

Perhaps one of the hardest tasks of widowhood is to communicate to other people the stage at which you have arrived. I find it much more important to communicate to others now my interior state of mind – to say simply but firmly, for example, 'I am very grateful for your concern – but I don't feel quite ready to date someone else', or 'I understand why you might think it would be more convenient for me to move, but I do find my house, garden and neighbours very comforting.'

When you are ready, and not before, you will feel the urge to move forward, to venture out, whether in terms of relationships, decisions regarding work or house, or making one of the 'journeys' that is so much a part of grief work. I have made journeys and I have stood still – in fact I have done a lot of standing (or sitting) still.

From my own experience and from talking to others I would say that the best sort of support one can offer someone immediately after bereavement is just to let them know you are there. The bereaved also want to know that the little steps of progress they have made have been noted and appreciated; 'I think you are doing very well' can make all the difference to their morale. The bereaved, above all, want encouraging: to be made to feel that from 'crawling along the bottom' they have made progress up and out. They also want permission to feel their grief and be allowed to express it. It is not particularly helpful to hear 'Are you back at work yet?' when all you feel like is crawling into bed and staying there for a year. It is not particularly helpful to hear about the 'stages' of grief from other people. Everyone moves through them at a different pace and in a different order.

The best thing is to acknowledge the bereaved person's feelings. 'It must be terrible for you, it must feel so lonely' is actually more consoling than 'Try and get yourself out more'. People unintentionally can say the most wounding or ridiculous things. Very often, it is for want of anything better to say. Language fails, and they resort to homilies: 'Time will heal'; 'Be thankful you've got the children'. It is as if they are saying you should be grateful for having anything left at all of your future. But it can be more difficult when people say nothing at all – carefully steering the conversation around the subject, avoiding mentioning the death. This is not acknowledging who you are, now. It is akin to staring right through you, as if you were the furniture.

*

If much of recovery has to do with standing up to other people's expectations, it has to do too with countering the many negative stereotypes of the widow that still amazingly prevail. One has to try and understand why in so many cultures, the widow is seen as in almost the same category as a witch or female demon. In the past few years I have personally encountered almost every one of the most commonly held assumptions: that she is rich, bawdy, shameless, crafty, poor, lustful and of course, merry. And it is not only folk-wisdom that would have it so. Even sophisticated contemporary writers use the figure of a widow to exemplify at once the most cunning and the most licentious – though with just a hint of 'piteous' thrown in. If woman in western society is split into opposing images of madonna/whore – the widow too incorporates some of that split. In *The Holy Living* Jeremy Taylor writes:

> Widowhood is pitiable in its solitariness and loss, but amiable and comely when it is adorned with gravity and purity, and not sullied with remembrances of the passed licence, nor with present desires of returning to a second bed.

These attitudes live on today, with the widow being a favourite prey of journalists. In an article in *Tatler* entitled *Widow Polish*, Gully Wells wrote sneeringly:

> To be widowed is to be sanctified. To be divorced is either to be ignominiously dumped . . . or to be a hell-hag and a marriage-wrecker . . . Either way, it is none too dignified.

Nor too profitable. The widow has it made: the saintly aura ('she was holding his hand when he died, you know'). The great man's name is hers for ever more: she is the sole guardian of his flame and his trust fund, plus she gets to enjoy the elegant independence that comes from a huge amount of money allied to the clout of an instantly recognizable name.

While this writer's resentment knows no bounds, another, Hugo Vickers, in the same feature, goes on to describe 'the dowager' in much the same scathing tones:

The dowager is, by definition, always more powerful than a mere wife. She has the name, the clout, the cachet and the loot. She is a truly liberated woman, her own master, answerable to no man and able to fulfil herself in whatever direction her fancy runs to. There's only one last thing to be said about Power Widows ... they *never* get married again. And who can blame them?

There is a viewpoint which is becoming increasingly fashionable today, that it is somehow glamorous to be a widow – that one wears widowhood like a designer label, rather like dark glasses or 'power suits'; that widowhood somehow spells 'allure'; that the widow is, à la Jackie Onassis or Yoko Ono, mega-rich, eternally young, remote and unobtainable: that she lives shrouded in her husband's legend. Some writers have gone even further and suggested with some malice and, no doubt, envy that there is such a thing as the 'professional' widow who cashes in on her husband's fame. No doubt there are a few widows (wives of celebrities) who appear to be in that category – but that may only be as viewed *from the outside*.

While these stereotypes might apply to a handful of extremely rich and famous widows like Jackie Onassis, Yoko Ono or the Queen Mother, they are so far removed from the average widow's reality as to be almost risible. Nor is any mention made of the often daunting responsibilities that many 'power widows' have to take on, maintaining their late husband's reputation or managing his money for example, or living up to a concept of the late man's greatness – which is probably the real reason why such widows often do not remarry. They cannot find another man as worthy – not in their own eyes, but in those of the world, and these sort of widows are acutely conscious of how the world views them. In that sense, they may be 'professional' widows, but only because they have never managed either to rid themselves of or to share all the world's expectations of them.

In the case of both Jackie Onassis and Yoko Lennon, we do not know the full extent of the upset and traumas they had to endure either during their marriages or afterwards. We know Kennedy was a relentless womanizer, John Lennon a neurotic verging on psychotic, if his biographer Albert Goldman is to be believed. It is simply assumed that money, name and position must ease the way. On the other hand, widows left with no legacy of work, name or fortune, might in one sense find it easier to carve out a future as their own woman. I speak as one who is very happy to have been left a magnificent collection of paintings, yet very aware that I have a huge responsibility to these paintings – to house and exhibit them to their best advantage and to keep Jacques' reputation always in circulation.

The widow may in the eyes of some be 'a truly liberated woman . . . answerable to no man and able to fulfil herself in whatever direction her fancy runs to'; but the reality probably is that she feels very much in charge of her late husband's reputation and is burdened with books, objects or even businesses she may want to be free of. I know of one young widow left a vast estate, antiques, and vintage cars worth millions, who has spent the last five years trying to free herself from the fortune-hunters and other hangers-on who continue to plague her. She is fearful to leave her large house and even take a short holiday, for in the past, when she has done so, people have moved in and helped themselves to anything they fancied. She has found a modicum of sanity and happiness by taking an ordinary job in a laboratory which has allowed her to build up some identity for herself.

It is not difficult to understand why resentment against a widow's seeming freedom should exist, when even in the most liberated and modern of partnerships a woman still often has to ask permission to spend her own money, take a separate holiday, or turn her mother-in-law down one Christmas. It is not difficult either to understand a man's fear of the woman who appears to be her own free agent who, unlike the single woman or even the divorcee, has perhaps appeared to be quite content to play side-kick for the greater part of her life and is now showing a surprising independence. There is a feeling that in showing such spirited independence and an ability to cope alone, the widow has in some way betrayed her husband.

I will never forget the relish with which one woman described to me the death of an elderly widower just nine months after he had lost his wife. There was more than a note of reproach in her voice as she said, 'Well, of course, he loved her very much and just couldn't live without her . . . but then, some people do seem to pine more than others . . .' We may express our disapproval of 'suttee' in this society (the former Hindu custom whereby a widow burnt herself to death on her husband's funeral pyre); but there still, to some extent, is a notion of 'emotional suttee' – the idea that no one has the right to recover too well, or cope too confidently. There are vestiges too of the idea that the widow has not only been greedy and undeserving in inheriting the fruits of her husband's labour (be it reputation or wealth), but that she has in some way contributed to his death (even when it was patently accidental or random as in the case of John Lennon). This goes half-way to explaining the vehemence with which Yoko Ono was represented as 'Bitch-on-Wheels' (notably in the Goldman book).

I have come to the conclusion that the malice aimed at widows is actually an expression of resentment at the fact that they are a category of women no longer under anybody's control. This is all a reflection of a culture that has no place, no real comparison, for the widow. My friend and colleague Mary Kenny pointed out that dispensable words at the end of a column of type are still known as 'widows' – again conveying the notion of something 'surplus'. Over the past few years I have begun to realize that 'widow avoidance' and other strange and hurtful attitudes I experienced were not specific to me, but widespread throughout many cultures and may well be universal, reflecting the fact that the widow is regarded as an anomaly. We may not, like the American Indians, cast the widow out of the tepee, but we certainly cold-shoulder her in other ways. We may not officially make her the village prostitute, as did some societies, but folk sayings imply that she is voraciously sexual. A widow is basically not allowed to just 'be' in her undefined state, as a Spanish proverb expresses: 'A buxom widow should get herself married or buried, or shut away in a convent.'

The widow is often represented as veiled, mysterious and shadowy, an erotic mingling of sex and death. Many popular sayings and proverbs express the sinister idea of the 'black widow', who is seen as the 'touch of death'. 'You must be wary how you marry a widow, for so you will be subject to have a death's head put often in your dish' (James Howell, *Familiar Letters Vol II*).

I am struck looking through the literature at how different the Old Testament's attitude is towards the widow, where a man is constantly enjoined to make the widow's lot a little easier: 'I caused the widow's heart to sing for joy' (Job XXIV – 13) and widowhood is seen as a state of special dignity and purity. It was only later that she came to be seen as essentially impure. In the Bible a widow is given legal protection (Exodus XXII – 21 and Deut. XXVII – 19). Her property cannot be taken from her by creditors; she cannot be denied any sum stipulated in her marriage contract; she must be supported by her husband's heirs, if destitute. Later rabbinical decrees further ruled that a bride cannot in her marriage contract surrender the lien which her claim on her dead husband's estate represented.

Paradoxically, as women's status rose, the widow was increasingly resented, and essentially by the most liberated women who had achieved economic parity with men. Once again, the protection offered to the weakest and most vulnerable under patriarchy was sharply withdrawn: women, above all, seemed to resent other women who looked as if they had achieved something for nothing. There is perhaps too resentment that the widow's loss should elicit general sympathy and consideration when others have suffered losses of equal magnitude which receive less recognition. The person who has been made redundant, given birth to a handicapped child or had a mastectomy has suffered an overwhelming loss and seen a future wiped out. I have had a lot of time to think about the curious and almost universal resentment expressed towards widows and have come to the conclusion that it goes even deeper than fear of the anomalous – the person between categories, the spider in the cracks – and must subconsciously be tied in with deeply held notions of the woman both as life and death bringer. It is eventually fear of women, of the feminine, distorted and writ large – which is why it is certainly bound up with sex.

Few expect to be young widows today, since modern medicine holds out a promise of longevity for everyone. That is probably one of the reasons why widowhood is now such a taboo subject. If the nineteenth century had a sentimentalized image of the widow in her weeds – the ultimate being Queen Victoria herself – living in either isolated dignity or eking out some humble existence – today society somehow blames her for surviving at all. She represents the ultimate let-down of modern life: the failure of modern technology. No wonder the glossies callously malign her as if she were guilty of some terrible crime. The 'crime' of course is outliving her man and possibly enjoying some of the fruits of his labours. I know that many widows feel 'survivor' grief – especially those widowed after a sudden illness or accident; whereas those whose partners died of cancer or a wasting disease also may have to grieve for the loss of the man as they knew him, and often the disintegration of the personality. Melanie Klein wrote of what she called 'the triumph over the dead' bereaved people feel, which they often turn into anger against themselves or others. Whereas others may see only the 'triumph', the widow herself, on the contrary, feels she has to atone – to justify her own existence – made doubly hard by the attitude of others.

It is assumed that widowers have a much easier time of it than widows – partly because of a man's greater ability to make a good living, and partly because popular wisdom has it that a single man is always more socially desirable than a single woman, and will be on everybody's invitation list. The widower is thus expected to be 'merrier' than the not-so-merry widow. To some extent this is borne out by the reality: many more widowers than widows re-marry – and within a much shorter period, too.

But widowers can share many of the problems of the widow: inability to come to terms with their loss, extreme loneliness, apathy and sometimes severe income loss. The widower left to cope with a young family is a case in point, or the widower who has nursed a terminally sick wife over a long period, leaving him drained of resources. For some, like one I

know who had watched his wife waste away from
cancer, it corresponded to a low point in his career.
Faced with a choice between re-training, redundancy
or early retirement, he chose the latter – only to find his
lack of goals and dwindling social life, now that he had
neither colleagues nor the strictures of work, left him
bored, apathetic and severely depressed. With the loss
of both his wife and his job he felt robbed of everything
meaningful in his life. His two daughters, both in their
early twenties, lived with him – but he felt unable
either to cope with their problems of jobs, boyfriends
or to accept any dependency on them. He felt his life
should after three years take a new direction but didn't
know how. He resented well-meaning friends' attempts
at match-making and thus turned down most invitations, becoming a bit of a recluse.

Widowers too – like all men in general – are less
ready to seek counselling or help. Tom had not seen a
bereavement counsellor, but one day, about a year
after his wife's death, he realized he had reached a
point of no return when he simply found himself
'going walk about', dazed and faint in a village about
fifteen miles from home (he presumed he had walked
there). Whereupon he decided to see his local doctor,
with whom he was able to talk about his feelings.

Three years on, he is thinking of seeing a counsellor
because he realizes he is 'stuck' in many areas. He feels
he needs advice about retirement, possible re-training
or part-time work, and a way of ridding himself of, in
his words, 'the shadow which is always with me'. To a
large extent this is guilt relating to conflicts that
existed in his relationship with his wife long before her
death and which he has not managed to acknowledge
or resolve.

It has been noted by many writers that the guilt and anger so often responsible for keeping a person 'stuck' in his or her bereavement follow the dissolution of an ambivalent relationship. Yet it would be difficult, I imagine, to find a relationship that had not been characterized by some degree of ambivalence. Wanting to see a counsellor is perhaps the first recognition and admission of these feelings.

I have not spoken to enough widowers to know whether they experience the same feelings as widows, but those I have spoken to have given me the impression that whereas widowers may suffer from the same loss of structure and confidence – since their identity is so rarely tied up solely in their partner – they often have to work alone to find a new confidence.

Since they are not stigmatized in the same way as widows, or thought to have the same 'spoiled identity' they have a much easier time constructing a new social identity. Whereas the widower of this world is deemed socially desirable the same rarely applies to the widow.

Chapter Nine

Haven or Hindrance?

'But she was home. She was grateful for that. Here she could be herself, live or die. Do nothing. Endure.'
                    Susan Hill, *In the Springtime of the Year*

To move or not to move house presents a major dilemma for most widows. Some, of course, are forced to do so from economic necessity, but many more feel pressured into doing so, regardless of whether there is the financial need or not. Many people make you feel that there is something very wrong in wanting to remain in the house where you have perhaps spent twenty or more years of your life. 'Are you going to move?' is one of the first and most frequent questions you hear after a bereavement, as if there is something almost obscene about staying where you are. At times I felt it was almost resentment being expressed at the fact that a woman on her own was continuing to live in a large house and was, more importantly, managing to cope pretty well. There is a feeling that people want you to reduce yourself – almost 'How dare she continue to live as if she were two?'

Feelings about making a move will fluctuate over time, and they vary from person to person. Many widows and widowers sell their homes not only because they hope to escape reminders of the past, in an attempt to create a new life, but because, without their partner, the house has lost its meaning for them, and they no longer feel about it in the same way. Your immediate instinct may be to up and go; but many widows say they regret the too-hasty decision taken in the first few months, and many admit to feeling that a move into something smaller can exacerbate the feeling that the family has broken up irreparably, because they no longer, for example, have the extra bedroom to lodge the grown-up child, or grandchild, or the space to entertain.

Your home has often taken many years to get together: it is an extension of your personality; and in my case I felt I had put a lot of myself into it. It is hard for someone who has not been left in this position to understand the reluctance to sell off everything you have worked for – and the sadness that comes with the thought of parting with those things which, after all, are a part of your life. It is not a question of acquisitiveness, or even of keeping up a standard of living, which almost inevitably drops with widowhood anyway. Playwright Alan Bennett's brilliant monologue by the widow in his *Talking Heads* series expresses most poignantly the feelings of a woman having to cope with selling her last sticks of furniture and living in one bleak room.

I did briefly think about selling the house and the cottage in Cornwall, but felt totally unequal to the task: traumatized and exhausted, I was patently not up to suffering another trauma of moving. The thought of 'reducing myself' filled me with despair. I had a large library, huge paintings and all the usual china and household objects one collects over twenty-five years. I was not ready to think about getting rid of any of them: in fact, I needed these possessions as a source of comfort: they were part of my identity.

Moving house represents a major upheaval when all

you want, at least in the early days, is peace and a calm haven. My feelings about moving have swung to and fro over the past few years as the following diary extracts reflect. On one occasion in 1989 I made an abortive attempt to move. I went to a very plush-looking estate agent in Hampstead and spent the day being driven around by a glamorous blonde looking at various overpriced flats. The effect was to make me realize that I was absolutely crazy to think of swapping my own comfortable, spacious home for these bijou cramped properties: that I was reacting to other people's pressure and was simply not ready for such a move.

I wander from room to room. Everything is in order – beautiful even – with the plants and flowers carefully arranged. Yes, the house is beautiful, but it seems to have no meaning these days. On other days, it is a haven. I walk through the door and feel a sense of calm, of security. I walk from my kitchen, down the steep stone steps into the little patio, my little wonderland, full of pots of pansies, geraniums, intertwined with climbing roses and nasturtiums, the grapevine and heavy, overhanging honeysuckle. This is my manageable corner of the world. Then I venture further, through the summerhouse and on to the lawn, and sit in the early evening cool and look at the poppies – poppies blowing in the wind scattering their petals, reminding me of Jacques' poppy paintings – the poppy, so evocative of the fragility of life, of spilled blood, of youth and beauty cut down. And I listen to the birds. I can pick out individual birdsong and think that some birds come specially each evening to sing to me. I even imagine childishly that one particularly lovely songster is Jacques in another incarnation.

On the days when I come battle-scarred from the city and battles with the traffic, tedious films and the hot dusty pavements full of pedestrians, the garden feels a virtual paradise. On others, when I haven't been into town and time hangs heavily, I wander round the garden sluggishly. Time changes meaning according to how much structure you have in your life. With empty hours you long to fill your time with purposeful activity and envy every whey-faced commuter heading for his mapped out day.

If you stay on in the house as I did, what tends to happen is that it gradually acquires a new meaning. The house where both Jacques and I used to work – he in his studio upstairs, and I downstairs, usually at the kitchen table – no longer smells of fresh oil paint or turpentine. But the paintings still hang in all the larger rooms and I still take visitors to the messy studio I have left intact. There was a danger it might become a virtual museum or even shrine and I was determined that this would not happen although there are reminders of Jacques everywhere. I now feel however, that the house has acquired something of a new character, because I have made some slight and subtle changes which have made the house more mine. I have repainted the outside and some of the interior. I have slightly changed the landscaping of the garden: a new 'edging' here, a new bank of lavender there, several new rose bushes and shrubs – but enough to make it feel mine. I think this is very important if you are staying in a house that you shared for many years with a partner. Redecorate a room, rearrange some furniture, and gradually the house, like you, will acquire a new identity. I am now thinking that if I stay put I will turn the studio into a library. I don't feel it necessary, as I did a year or so ago, to keep every old carton, jam jar and squeezed-out paint tube. I am gradually able to discard parts of the past, but there is so much I want to hold on to, and why should that be wrong?

At one point I did temporarily rent a flat in North London:

May 1989

> I am trying to close some of the doors to the past and open new ones to the future – but it is so hard. I have put Fuchsia Cottage on the market. I have also rented a small one-bedroom flat in Hendon (in the street where I used to go to school) in a shabby block full of old ladies (probably widows like myself). The flat itself is nice and bright and airy, newly decorated by its Chinese owner, Mr Yan. Mina and I are supposedly going to share it – though she has moved all her stuff in, and I

will only sleep there one or two days a week. I
am pleased. My mother will be able to pop in
and Mina will have the family on hand. It is
back to roots.

This did not last long. When there I craved my house
and couldn't wait to get back. At other times I was all
too aware of its emptiness:

> I feel terribly sad, anguished even, as I sit
> alone in the big house over Bank Holiday,
> with all the lilac in bloom, daisies on the lawn
> and cats sprawled at my feet. Where has it all
> gone? I wonder – all those years of children's
> laughter, family holidays, big meals and
> outings? With Mina and Elias gone I am really
> alone – going through the empty nest
> syndrome, as well as bereavement.

I remained very torn about whether or not to sell the
big old house. As it was, the recession intervened, and I
found myself, like many other home-owners, both
unable to sell and reluctant to let go of a once-valuable
home for what would have to be far below its normal
price. Because of the recession too my twenty-five-
year-old son, having completed a second degree in
archaeology at university, eventually moved back into
the house. With jobs for archaeologists scarce, he had
decided to embark on a new business venture.
Consequently, the studio I had planned to turn into
my library became his office, and once again the house
took on a new character.

I have, however, started to make plans for better
days, when I will eventually let go of the house,

though I do not feel any real urgency to make a decision at this moment. This represents, I think, the difference between where I am *now* in terms of emotions, and where I was three or four years ago, when I felt obliged to precipitate some change artificially. I am much more capable of living in the present and even visualizing a future. The past has definitely lost some of its hold.

I have become aware, too, over the years how difficult it is for a woman to cope single-handed with the maintenance of an old house. In the first few months after Jacques died came the dawning realization that a number of items in my house had died a death too. Many widows tell me that immediately after a death they become aware that simply everything needs fixing. This is probably partly because you are spending more time at home and are forced to become aware of your immediate surroundings, and partly because of actual neglect which happens when you are totally preoccupied with illness. Partly too, it is because in a partnership maintenance is often done invisibly and taken for granted, and you are simply unaware of this aspect of the division of labour: appliances get fixed, light bulbs changed and blocked drains cleared. Jacques had been a very good mechanic, carpenter and builder, and I had left those things to him. I cannot recall our ever using outside help for home maintenance. I am ashamed to admit I literally could not even change a light bulb in the very beginning, and sometimes had to sit there in darkness rather than ask my neighbour and appear utterly foolish; though after a few months I put aside my almost irrational fear of electricity and managed to screw in my first one.

Now I seemed to spend much of the time on the phone to builders, plumbers and maintenance men. The extra tasks not only came as something of a shock, they were also extremely tiring and expensive. I seemed to spend hours hunting through the Yellow Pages. I suspected that every builder or service man I called out would suddenly up his prices, sensing a desperate woman alone; and I didn't quite know how to deal with that as I was literally, with taps dripping, and roofs leaking, at their mercy.

I remember one central heating repair man who came to service my boiler and told me that a major part needed replacing. After he had replaced the part for a great deal of money the boiler plainly was malfunctioning and giving me even more problems. He then said I needed an even more expensive replacement, which I agreed to and which once again lasted only a few days. He then told me that I would need the entire boiler replaced, which he could do at the 'special price' of approximately £2000. At this point something told me I needed a second opinion! Fortunately through the Yellow Pages I hit upon an honest repairman, a real craftsman, who had been in the business with his father for many years. After thoroughly testing the boiler he told me there was absolutely nothing wrong with it except that a defective part had been fitted in the first place which caused a knock-on effect. The first man had been belligerent and downright nasty and I could not face confronting him directly, though I knew he had caused me a lot of aggravation as well as tremendous expense; so I asked the second repairman if he would call him direct and tell him what he had found, and try to reach some kind of settlement for me. This he kindly did and I was spared the cowboy's bad language and aggression. Finding a practical mediator of this kind is a godsend for any widow who doesn't feel quite up to dealing with this kind of incident – which is not uncommon.

I was of course experiencing what every woman who lives alone has to contend with: I had not realized quite how protected I had been in my marriage. At one point, I seemed to be a target for every passing cowboy and hustler. A succession of dubious characters would arrive on my front door step and offer their services – ranging from roof tiling to tree surgery (one unsolicited tree surgeon actually started to saw down a tree until I rushed out and stopped him, whereupon he tried to charge me for the two branches he had removed). At first I would think that these were genuine acts of helpfulness until I realized they had sussed from someone that a young widow was living on her own in a big house which could provide a source of income for them. The feeling of being preyed upon was to stay with me for quite a while. I was in no condition at that point to act upon the world, to be assertive in any way, though I was gradually to learn how to send out messages that the 'poor widow' was not there for them to take advantage of.

It only gradually dawned on me that I had to take total responsibility for every decision at home. This applied even to the purchase of new household appliances. Unusual though it may seem I had never made these kinds of decisions. Soon after Jacques died both the vacuum cleaner and the washing machine packed up altogether. Jacques had normally seen to the purchase of major items like that. When they all went at once I dreaded having to buy new ones. Since they were costly items, and I felt in no condition to decide anything, I chose a shop that was holding a sale of electrical goods – and since I was totally unable to judge the relative merits of any of the machines I opted for simplicity and ease and chose the two best-known brand names, with the simplest operating instructions and the longest guarantees. I also chose a way of paying for them (by postdated cheques) that was not exactly hire purchase but was not too hard on the pocket either. When I finally had them delivered and the washing machine installed I felt an immense sense of pride at my purchases in that I was starting to make the household *mine* instead of ours.

Looking back over my diary now it is clear how I have made the emotional journey from seeing the house as a safe haven to workplace to something more neutral that can expand, contract or change with time. The animal feeling of wanting a dark hole to crawl into where you can lick over wounds at first prevails. As you start to see a glimmer of light and those wounds heal, everything around you, all the finest details and familiar objects, appear with a new intensity: for the time being, they *are* the meaning in your life. Finally you dare to venture further afield and the primitive animalism you temporarily reverted to starts to fade as the world and greater objectivity take over.

Chapter Ten

Out of the Shadows

'Embrace the emptiness and know that you will not always feel this way, and that just by holding still and feeling it you will begin to fill it with the warmth of self acceptance.'

Robin Norwood, *Women Who Love Too Much*

Mourning seems to be equally divided between holding still and being very quiet, between regrouping your forces or energies and making a surge forward. In order to move forward, you have to stand still, give yourself a chance not to have to make any decisions: to turn off all the lights for a while, and allow your pain to speak to you. During this time, you are so extremely vulnerable that it is best to cocoon yourself and steer clear of any people or experiences that can bruise you or re-open wounds. This includes the books you read, the music you listen to, and the friends you seek advice from. Like someone in intensive care, you need to be very quiet and steer clear of infection and possibly have someone – a counsellor or therapist – to support you through these times.

Post-bereavement depression is one of the most difficult of all depressions to shake off. There is, after all, a good reason for the depression. Without the future you had to look forward to, life appears to have lost all meaning. A leaden inertia weighs upon you and each day seems as unendingly grey as the last – an ordeal to be got through . . . You have to get used to the long periods of silence, a silence interrupted in your imagination only by the ghostly slam of the front door at the time he used to come home, his footsteps on the stairs, or the creak of the chair he used to sit in. Long silences when the phone never rings and you feel it will never ring again. Before, I had welcomed silence as a relief from all the hectic clatter surrounding me. Now there was nothing but silence. It would be dishonest to pretend I did not have to contend with the blackest bouts of depression during all that time when I was trying to come back into the world. I used dream therapy, hypnotherapy, diet, exercises, will power and work and everything else to keep going – but depression was bound to hit and hit it did!

For me the most difficult time of all was about six months after Jacques' death. At that stage I went through a real crisis, and this was after I had proved I could cope with legal matters, get the children back on track and myself back to work. I was doing well: I felt reasonably cheerful and energetic and then, suddenly, I felt I no longer wanted to cope. I was hit by total despair, the feeling that nothing would ever change for me. Apathy descended on me, I no longer had any desire to work, to see anyone, or to keep the household routine. A feeling of utter meaningless mess hit me. I even stopped visiting the cemetery, which had always been a comfort. Now there was no comfort. The reality dawned on me. I was a widow – but how was I to break the spiral of depression and blackness?

A remark from a friend helped: 'If I were in your shoes I wouldn't be coping so well, I'd have pulled the duvet over my head and stayed there for three months. I'd treat myself as if I were ill. You *are* ill.' She was right; I was coping too well, my daily routine was masking emotions that demanded to be released. I realized I was angry at being left alone with all this responsibility. I went again to the cemetery and raged at Jacques. 'How could you do this to me?' For a few days I hated him and everyone else. Then miraculously the storm passed.

I was experiencing the 'grand crisis' of mourning. Some, like me, experience it at six months, others at a year, others many years later and some not at all. But many widows have described this crisis to me and how difficult it was to extricate themselves from it. In my journal I wrote:

> There are days when you feel so low, so set back, that unless you consciously make a commitment to life, it would be easy just to stop eating, smother myself under a pillow, or jump under a train.

Often, it's extreme tiredness that brings it on. It takes a long time to adjust physically to being one person. For the first year or so I was running around like a chicken with its head cut off, trying, as one person, to do everything that two had done. I would let nothing go, whether it was running errands for the children (and they had become very used to using me as secretary, rescuer, messenger, library book getter, researcher, interviewer, fixer of all kinds), trying to see my mother and other family members, and keeping up with friends. It never occurred to me just to stand still and let life revolve around me: I was still feverishly fitting in with what I thought was everyone's expectations of me.

Something that does not seem to shift for a very long time is what C. S. Lewis called 'the inertia of grief'. How apt that phrase is. How difficult it is to find the motivation to accomplish even the simplest of tasks. Take something like selling a car. For almost two years Jacques' car sat in the garage – unused, untaxed, MOT expired. I had every intention of selling it (it was far too big), but instead this awful inertia took over. It meant advertising it, answering calls, then finding another, smaller car to replace it.

For weeks, months and then years it sat in the open garage gathering dust. I just couldn't find the mental energy to tackle it, and there were several other tasks in this category: things that needed doing around the house; finances that needed reorganizing. It took almost two years before I got round to any major reorganizing jobs – and then I inevitably needed a push from someone. With the car, it was the builders – working belatedly on the exterior of the house they offered to buy it and find me another. On closer examination, however, they found that the chassis had rusted and the offer was withdrawn. So the car continued to sit in the garage as a symbol of some protective presence. But that was all right: at least I recognized it for what it was. Finally moss and mould grew up the window-panes.

I was not too proud to realize it was now virtually worthless and that I would have to *pay* somebody to take it away. In the fourth year of my bereavement, one of my son's friends sold us a little VW Polo for practically nothing; it had been sitting in his driveway for years but was still in good nick. My son welcomed it as a runaround car, now that he had started his own business, one which necessitated a lot of travelling. Again, circumstances rather than feelings, determined the action – but emotionally I knew I was ready for it, and on the day the scrap-metal dealers towed the old car away I took myself out so as not to be there when they came – and felt quite pleased to see the little friendly silver Polo sitting in the driveway when I returned.

Part of the inertia represents unresolved guilt feelings. I have realized that bereavement and grieving create little holes in the social fabric and people just want to close them – plug them up as soon as possible. You may feel that people implicitly, if not explicitly, blame you for your husband's death. This is particularly common with those who have lost their partner from a terminal illness. It is human nature to want to apportion 'blame' – and when the illness has been sudden and rapidly fatal there is a tendency to look back over every moment of one's long relationship for 'beginnings', for some precipitant. The mind likes neat categories – and will not accept that there may, in fact, have been no reason for the illness – other than genetic in-built flaw. One of Jacques' few relatives that I had met had died, in fact, of the very same cancer at precisely the same age, pointing perhaps to some inherited genetic pre-disposition.

In my bad moments I would go on tormenting myself – going back over all the old photographs to see if I could spot tiny changes in the way Jacques looked. Was he thinner here or there? Did he look a bit grey there, or was it my imagination? It was only when I literally screamed at myself: 'STOP! What are you doing? Why don't you wear a hairshirt and flagellate yourself?', that I realized what guilt was doing. At this point I actually forbade my thoughts to wander over the imaginary time the cancer began. How could one ever know?

You feel after death rather like you feel after giving birth: you over-react to everything – from the indifferent shop girl who tells you to look for your own size 10 to the mother who smacks her child in the post office queue. You cry a great deal – and it helps if you allow for this overflow of feeling. As I wrote then:

> I seem to cry so easily at everything. I have just watched a 'Forty Minutes' documentary called 'Who Will Win Jeanette?' about a seventeen-year-old who 'chooses' the American couple she will give her baby to. I wept buckets. Everyone's loss becomes my own: this is the effect of bereavement.

The feelings of panic, anxiety and depression may be so severe at times, that you begin to fear you are going insane. In my case it could take as little as a thoughtless remark, however kindly meant, especially one that reactivates half-submerged feelings of guilt. I remember taking a Russian visitor sightseeing in Windsor some time after Jacques died. She suddenly stopped in front of an antique shop in Eton and remarked on an ornate mirror in the window. She then asked me how long the dressing-table mirror in our guest room had been cracked. I was a little embarrassed, as I thought I had skilfully disguised the crack, but I felt even worse as she went on to explain that in Russia a cracked glass usually meant a death in the family. At that moment I was not only gripped by giddiness but by all the darkest kinds of superstition. I racked my brains. When had it cracked? Had I been aware of it at the time? Who had done it? Worst of all – had it been me?

Had I inadvertently killed my husband? Mercifully I remembered that our help (something of a 'klutz', forever banging into things) had slammed the Hoover into it – and with this memory, my sanity and balance returned. All this is to demonstrate just how easily one can be overcome by unreason, self-torment and guilt. Somewhere in the deepest recesses of the mind – especially when you have lost someone from a terrible illness – lingers that small suspicion that somehow you might have actually caused it, and it only takes the smallest suggestion to bring all those guilt feelings into play.

At a certain stage of grieving (and no one can determine when, for it is different for everyone) you may suffer intense paranoia, or something verging on it, a feeling that the world generally is hostile and failing to comprehend your innermost feelings. Thus the incident with the poppies which I recorded in my journal in the summer of 1989 reflects my feelings of being 'got at'.

> Strange how everyone seems intent to kill off my memories. Now the gardener, in his zeal to tidy the garden, digs up half my ornamental poppies and chops off their heads. Caught mid-action, scythe in hand, I scream at him to stop and nearly frighten the poor man to death. Little does he know that it is my memories of these poppies that bring back Jacques and his paintings. I am both furious and sad.

A similar thing happened with the huge fuchsia bushes growing on the patio of our cottage in

Cornwall. The agent, mis-interpreting my instructions to clear the weeds in the front patio, ordered someone to brutally chop down the beautiful ten foot high fuchsia to about a foot. It looked like a massacre when I arrived; I was devastated – particularly when a neighbour in an off-hand way said 'I don't know what you're going on about; they've needed cutting back for years.' No remark could have been more callous to me in my hypersensitive state. 'Did she,' I wrote in my journal, 'understand the memories the bell-shaped flowers carried with them? Other people neither care for nor understand your memories: how could they? – and that's why they can ride roughshod over them.' Looking back, this accurately mirrors my raw feelings of the time and many widows I have spoken to have echoed this – the feeling they have been grossly misunderstood by the people around them.

It is precisely when you start to become over-whelmed by these sort of feelings – which largely denote the sort of impotence one associates with being a small child – that you have to take the action I call making a commitment to life. Depression, impotence and frustration can only be overcome by exerting some measure of control over your own life – taking the reins again and saying 'this is what I want'. Every time you make a choice for yourself, you feel better. Desperation comes from the feeling of being 'acted upon' rather than acting. That is why I urge anyone going through the terrible inertia or apathy of bereavement to force themselves to take action – any action, however small – at every opportunity. Rather than sitting there staring at the four walls, force yourself to take a walk. Unable to decide whether to buy six apples or three oranges at your local supermarket, force yourself to buy half a dozen daffodil bulbs instead, or alternatively buy yourself a new record, a book, or even a bar of soap. Even if the actions seem fairly disconnected and meaningless at the time, you will at least have made a choice. One of the best pieces of advice I ever received and one which I didn't fully understand at the time was to 'make sure that you dance at every wedding'. That means, never miss out on an opportunity to celebrate something – even if the celebration is something intensely personal, having meaning only to you. Light a candle if you feel like it; dress up just for yourself. Ritualizing your life will gradually help you find your way back into the world. We all need symbols which represent life at its fullest and most joyous.

Everyone of course has to find her own way. The 'act of faith' I performed was buying a beautiful silver and black taffeta ballgown I had seen in the window of a local boutique. I had no ball to go to and no partner, but I liked the way I looked in it and it enabled me to envisage a time when someone might invite me to dance again. So I bought it, put it away in the attic room and from time to time went up to look at it as a symbol of everything I would hopefully become. And it worked; it was the beginning of a change in me – though I still have not worn it to this day.

Even if you don't buy a ballgown – a positive affirmation like 'I will be happy' or 'I am beginning to feel better' is a start. I am a great believer in positive affirmations, and I use them every day. It continued every time I made a decision to buy something new (from the Hoover to a new shrub for the garden) or engage in a new activity (from the writing of that sit-com in my first year of mourning to the tap-dancing classes I started to take in my second year).

You have to accept that in the first couple of years there is a lot of travelling backwards: indeed it often seems like one step forward, two back. And there is nothing like another funeral for bringing back the most painful memories. After my own bereavement there seemed to be a spate of deaths, including one older member of the family; but none so tragic as a close friend who died from cancer of the breast after just six months. She had been a particularly vivid presence and I had helped cook for her towards the end. Her fight for life had been almost a repetition of Jacques', except she had willingly gone into a hospice in the last weeks. I had submitted myself to a close-up of the same horrors as before – perhaps thinking *this* time there had to be hope.

> Suddenly another star has gone from your firmament: another light goes out, and one loss brings back another. She was buried very near to Jacques. I couldn't keep my eyes off his tombstone (on which I had placed champagne roses just before) as her coffin was lowered and I tossed earth on it with the other mourners. 'I have followed too many coffins,' I thought as I walked behind it to the grave, that slow dream-like walk, and listened to the rabbi utter the familiar words.

Every funeral brings out the emotions anew. I was invited to the memorial service of Sir Laurence Olivier in my professional capacity. I found myself almost morbidly attracted to such events for a while: perhaps trying to locate something I had lost with Jacques.

I sit in St Ermin's Hotel an hour before the
thanksgiving service alone with my thoughts.
I think about celebrating the life of a great
artist. I cross the road and join the guests at
the North door of the Abbey. Once inside,
seated I gaze at the Gothic heights above, the
illustrious around me and all the pomp and
pageantry of Lord Olivier's thanksgiving
service – I think of it as of my own memorial
service to Jacques. How he too would have
loved the colours and splendour, the trumpets
and the choirs and the good and beautiful
turning out to honour him. We both loved
Alec Guinness – and I think of this as his
mellifluous tones fill the Abbey with grace,
elegance, simplicity and beauty. We all weep
for one beautiful talented man – and again I
think of Jacques.

It very often feels as if you have made no progress
whatsoever; but I did manage to discover ways of
coping with the old feelings when they came back, as
they so often did, on birthdays, anniversaries or when
confronted with other deaths. I found that if I could
capture the 'girl within' I could extricate myself from
the worst feelings of despondency and desolation. I
had to keep reminding myself that 'the girl that was'
never dies – that she is always there waiting to be
invoked like some marvellous spirit. Dancing, poetry,
and later painting, were all to play their part. At other
black moments I have found that forcing myself to do
either something intensely physical (like digging over
a patch of garden) or something that requires great
concentration – like pen and ink drawing – also works.

At times it has been something more mundane like chopping up vegetables to make a soup which has got me out of my depression. Cooking for yourself means that you are nurturing yourself, and it is very important to find the ability to do this – to be able to draw comfort from yourself.

Comforting yourself is perhaps the most important thing you have to do after a loss of any kind. Very often there is no one else to offer you support: you have to find it from within. Therapists refer to this process in several ways: re-'parenting' yourself is one of them – learning to become your own nurturer.

How does one 'nurture' oneself? Starting at the most simple level, get yourself something nice to eat. The occasional splurge on a bundle of the finest asparagus or a few ounces of smoked salmon were my own favourite treats. Luxuries, perhaps, but you deserve them.

'Flower therapy' is another way. Once a week I would splash out on an armful of my favourite flowers: to my mind, not a luxury, but a necessity. If nobody sends you flowers, send yourself some – even if all you can afford is a small bunch of violets. I have always used flowers as a therapy. I remember when I was first married feeling rather alone in New York in the winter, and going out to buy armfuls of flowers to fill our sparsely furnished, fifth-floor walkup. I am a great one for filling any small space with greenery and colour. If you don't have a garden, you could do it on a balcony, or even buy some flowering indoor plants and mass them in one corner. I am convinced that the colour and scent of flowers has a healing and soothing quality which affects our mood (which is, of course, the theory applied in aromatherapy). Apart from the visual appeal, there may be a more scientific basis to this than is imagined, as plants are known to exert a powerful effect upon human behaviour.

If, like me, you work from home or live above the shop, it is important to find a space or room that you put aside simply for relaxation. I have one room which is furnished in shades of white and beige where I go for my 'tranquillity fix'. It is the room where I put on a record, read certain books (I never read anything associated with work in there) and spend much of my time just gazing out of the window. It is the room which allows me to escape from the rest of my everyday life, from clutter, bills, letters and reminders of all my responsibilities.

Other ways of pampering yourself and finding some kind of comfort and spiritual respite include soaking in a hot bath, spending time with enjoyable people, and I stress *enjoyable* – someone who makes you laugh, or seeing a film or a show. I have always found that I can lift even my blackest moods by choosing a lively piece of entertainment, either a good rousing musical or something so engrossing that it completely takes you out of yourself. It is important to select carefully because the wrong film or play can do just the opposite and plunge you into even worse depression. Everyone has their escapist favourites: for me it is anything to do with tap-dancing or *Gone With The Wind*: *Oklahoma* does it for me, too. Only you of course can gauge your mood: for this reason, it is a good idea not to book seats in advance, but to go to something as the mood takes you.

Comforting yourself should not only be reserved for moments of deepest despair: it is an on-going process that should begin from the moment you wake up to the last thing at night (times when you feel especially in need of consolation). Much of your feeling of apathy or depression stems from the sense of internal and external chaos. Feelings are so heightened, you dare not have them: nothing can be taken for granted. You live each moment on the edge of a volcano: is it any wonder your system shuts down while it awaits a new ordering of your world?

Any loss, and especially death, means the loss of structure and order – and it is important to find a new order even if it is not the same one as before. That is why, re-establishing a routine, any routine, is perhaps the most comforting thing you can do. After the chaotic first few months I gradually fell into a set routine in the mornings. At about 7 a.m. I would go downstairs to make my early morning cup of tea, let the cat out, or in – take the tea upstairs with the newspapers and go back to bed to have a fifteen-minute read before my bath. Jacques had always brought me my early morning cup of tea, and it was a long time before I could get used to doing it myself.

Having a bath made me feel my day had actually started, instead of that amorphous grey feeling that every minute, every hour runs into the next and that time has no meaning. Even re-establishing a simple routine of reading a newspaper, writing a few letters, doing half an hour's shopping, cooking something simple, tidying up and watching the news on television helps you to regain a sense of structure. As I remarked in my diary:

> I seem to spend forever sweeping crumbs from one corner of the kitchen to another: tidying, mopping-up, re-arranging, putting a

fork here, a dirty cup there – pulling up dead
leaves from plants – all this obsessive tidying
has to do with my need for order in at least
three or four square feet of my life. My
kitchen has become a ship's galley: never
particularly houseproud before, I now live in
fear of one outsize grain of rice on the floor, an
evil-smelling sink, or dingy dishcloths –
which would betray a certain tiredness or
collapse of spirit in me.

Weekends take particular planning – whereas before
you more or less took your family-centred activities for
granted. I think part of my Saturday 'doom and gloom'
derives from my childhood when I was forced to go to
synagogue by my father. To this day, I invariably wake
up with a bad headache on a Saturday, and although
this is supposed to be a day of spiritual repose and
calm, I go around with a feeling of depression. By
Sunday, my mood has changed – and I wake up at least
with a feeling of resolve: my resolutions may not
amount to much, but they renew my energy. I am
going to do two things: I am going to read the Sunday
papers and then go for a run. The latter is often a
euphemism for a fast walk, interspersed with a little
bout of running. As I approach my driveway, I put on a
last spurt so that at least I will impress the neighbours
since I am all togged out in tracksuit, running shoes
and headband. I come inside sweating and breathless
with a small sense of achievement.

Then I decide whether to ring one of the 'odd bods' like
myself – one of my single friends who also might just
be floating around at a loose end at weekends, invite
them over for lunch or tea, or get on a train to London

and do something (rare) or (rarer still) take off on a trip. Every empty weekend I run through the same possibilities but usually end up doing the handwashing or writing a letter as I remember with heavy heart the Sunday routine Jacques and I had, when we would often visit the local nursery, lug home dozens of plants which we would then both spend the afternoon planting. There was an area of the garden close to the kitchen, which I called 'My Wonderland', a lovely patio crammed full of plants and tubs, the only untameable area of the garden. I was particularly proud of it when it was a jumble of a million busy lizzies, pansies and petunias, with thick tumbling hedges of honeysuckle, roses and lavender filling the evening air with their heady scent. 'Look at my Wonderland,' I would say to Jacques, opening the back door for him to catch a glimpse and sniff the mingled perfumes, and each week he would pander to my childish greed for yet more flowers as we wheeled our cart round the nursery till it was almost too heavy to push.

Gradually I learned to accept the changes: in the interim period I persuaded friends to substitute for Jacques and take me to the garden centre. I attempted, in other words, to maintain the same routine. It took perhaps three to four years before I finally broke with all the old habits and did something entirely new. I am aware only now of how much I clung to the old routines for safety. The compulsive sweeping, cleaning and gardening were all part of my fight to retain some control over my life: I was clinging to the deadwood – at least until new green shoots started to grow.

*

One of the worst things about the death of somebody very close is the feeling of total abandonment. You really do at times experience a feeling of being 'orphaned' – of being a lost soul – of there being no place for you in the world any more. This feeling can be totally overwhelming. It may come even after a period when you feel you have made great strides forward and have learnt to stand on your own two feet and have an immense pride of doing so. Sudden regression, which happens to everyone who mourns, can occur any time and may leave you feeling helpless and disappointed.

After two years of being on my own, I felt quite comfortable and secure. I could deal with most day-to-day eventualities: I was making a good living, had a reasonable social life, and everything seemed pretty much on track. Then the unexpected and disturbing happened: there was a series of strange and upsetting coincidences. They began one terrible evening after I had returned from the theatre and found myself locked out of the house: the latch had been mysteriously put down from the inside. I called a neighbour who climbed in with a ladder and opened the door. I got into bed a little shaken, only to be aroused by a phone call with nothing but heavy breathing on the other end. Half an hour later there was another, and another and another. This was to begin a terrifying period of mysterious harassment calls which ended in my having to go ex-directory. The phone would ring every few seconds and always there would be just breathing. These calls had a devastating effect on me: I suddenly felt vulnerable, violated within my own home, and I dreaded it every time the phone rang. I felt almost contaminated, as if there were some sinister force out

there trying to damage me. Most of all I felt vulnerable
and frightened. It could have been anyone who had
ever read my columns. Did I have an enemy out there?
British Telecom told me that in their experience it was
rarely a stranger and that in the majority of cases, it
was a woman. The idea of some deranged woman out
there with me continually on her mind was conducive
to paranoia.

Eventually when my number was changed the
problem was solved, but there was no doubt that it
had added to my feeling of being totally unprotected. I
was brought to a state of near nervous breakdown by
these calls. At the same time I had briefly to go into
hospital for a minor operation: unfortunately a
secondary infection meant I had to take a high dose of
antibiotics which inevitably made me feel very low.
This, plus the enormous pressure put on me at work to
cover the Christmas and New Year period, invariably
made me feel even more depressed, since not only was
this the time of traditional jollity, which I had never
much relished, but the time of Jacques' death and all
the recurring memories.

Each year I made a charity lunch or dinner on the
anniversary to raise money for the National Society for
the Prevention of Cruelty to Children.

> The run-up to the end of the year has been
> exhausting: this year I was more ambitious
> than last: even with the NSPCC party (last
> year soup and sandwiches, this, a three-
> course meal for sixty). I am aware that I have
> tried to function as two people – and my body
> is feeling it. I have been in London every day
> this week: one day for the *New Woman* party –

soaked to the skin afterwards in a flimsy velvet party dress, desperately trying to hail a non-existent taxi on Oxford Street. Then a number eight bus which took me within half a mile of Paddington – again soaked. Sometimes you feel you are battling against all the elements – and there is no one to meet you at the station the other end: no one to make you a cup of tea when you finally get home. I want to scream, but there is no one to hear me but the cat.

Again I was trying to be both mother and father to my children, remembering all the matinee treats I had taken the children to in the past. Just a little Christmas alone with my son was probably not the right thing. Too much time to feel inadequate.

Everything conspired to make me feel like a football kicked around a pitch – or a little boat pitching in a rough sea. Christmas is always tough for the bereaved – but particularly so for me because of the anniversary of Jacques' death. I was at my lowest ebb. The 'Why is there no one there for me?' feeling grew. I am sure all women who live on their own – whether by chance or necessity – must have it from time to time; and it is very difficult not to give way to it and try instantly to recruit a new someone (male of course) – a 'rescuer' in other words. This of course is another form of infantile regression. We are going back to those hopeless feelings of abandonment and impotence we felt as babies. Perhaps because I endured separation from my mother as a very young child during the war I am particularly prone to suffer fear of abandonment. I must resist these feelings strenuously and remember that I have made great strides, that I am a strong independent woman, that I must not be knocked for six by unfortunate circumstances.

My advice to other women suffering similar set-backs is to try and scrutinize the feelings of helplessness: try to remember when you first felt them – for they undoubtedly derive from a much earlier period. Try too, to take every practical measure to ensure your health and safety are not being jeopardized. I, in fact, organized a rota of friends to come and stay with me over that bad period. Any form of company helps even if it can't be your closest friends. It is amazing how just hearing the sound of someone's voice can dissolve the fears. Try too to get on with everyday life to the best of your ability. It helps, too, to turn your feelings of helplessness and despair to anger – sometimes even to mentally rehearse a confrontation with your victimizer.

Regression can occur any time, any place, especially when you get a flash of the past giving you that 'where did it all go' feeling so familiar to the bereaved. Thus I wrote:

> Going back over your life without your partner can be a very sad experience. Some dying people are said to see their whole life flashing in front of them: bereavement makes you see your past life in photographic fixes. Suddenly a scene is conjured up – the girl or wife or young mother that was. You want it frozen in time: you want to step back into it, start again, not have the nightmarish bits happen. It is very much 'stop the world, I want to get off'. It is like delving into your dreams: the feeling lingers – it colours your

waking hours – yet you reach out and cannot really grasp them. These are my dreams and echoes from the past. I see snapshot images all of a sudden of the young mother wheeling the pram, of Jacques carrying the 'Moses basket' with a tiny Elias inside, of golden times on Cornish beaches when the kids were small. Where did it all go? I know I will never have it again. It is this realization of the passage of time – of the death of so many things – that brings the greatest sadness of all.

Eventually, for me, the crisis came to an end, calm was restored and I was able to write:

The darkest period has passed: I feel something oppressive being lifted and as I look out into the garden early in the morning from my kitchen window and catch a gold-pink sunrise I know that all is well in my world again. Periods of light and dark fluctuate – one has constantly to renew faith and hope in the future, especially after taking a battering.

Chapter Eleven

Stepping Out

'He that would woo a maid must feign, lie and flatter, but he that woos a widow must down with his britches and at her.'

Folk saying

It is not often appreciated that shock, loss and depression can dampen libido, or in some cases kill it altogether. I have encountered very few widows who have fitted the 'lusty' label – at least, not those recently bereaved. On the contrary, many have fought shy of sex for the first few years – some finding the thought of sharing a bed with another man a 'betrayal' of their late husband, others that their new activities leave them very little time and energy even to think about it. In my own case, I know that sexual feeling dwindled almost to nothing in the first year, was revived temporarily during a 'flurry' of dating during the second year, and with the reality of my new life and growth of identity in the third year, settled down to a lower level than before. It was almost as if I had replaced sex as the centre of my being with the new necessities of making a living, taking on heavy responsibilities and forming relationships of many different kinds.

Now, after four years, I can admit to feeling 'normally sexy' – though there is no desperation or urgency there, and much is channelled into other creative outlets like dancing and painting. In this sense I am no different from any other single woman today –

whether she is twenty-five or sixty-five – who is certainly less prone to engage in casual sex than she was ten years ago. This is not to say that I did not crave touch and affection, and never more so than immediately after Jacques died and I was alone in the big house. But since, in England especially, we confuse touch with sex, or think that the first immediately has to lead to the other, the longed-for hugs and caresses that come with no strings attached are few and far between. Indeed many women may go to bed with a virtual stranger simply in order to feel themselves touched at last – to get some skin-to-skin contact. Probably this explains why the most enduring stereotype of the widow is as lust incarnate – perpetually 'on heat' and dying for a man's sexual advances.

Many men still, unfortunately, tend to believe this myth, and every young widow will have at least one story to tell of a man (often an old friend, or even husband of a friend) who makes a sudden and unwelcome sexual advance. I certainly noticed a new light in several husbands' eyes whenever they had a chance to be alone with me: the arm round the shoulder or waist was not quite so innocent as before; and once or twice I encountered behaviour that verged on downright sexual harassment. If confronted the man in question would invariably defend himself with, 'But I thought you wanted it. It must be so hard for you having to do without it now.' In other words, 'I am offering to do you a favour . . . be grateful.'

Far from finding this kind of behaviour flattering, the widow is likely to find it almost an assault on her being, and does not always know how to defend herself against it, especially if she has been brainwashed into believing she ought to feel 'sexy'; that sex equals love and comfort - regardless of where it is coming from. There is a commonly held idea that if you have had a long intimate relationship with someone, a hiatus without sex must be very difficult to manage. In fact, the opposite is probably true, but people tend to project their own fantasies and secret desires on to the widow, especially because she seems to fit no category. She does not, unless she is still tied to the past, belong to anybody except herself.

For a while my sexuality was channelled into the huge surges of energy I needed to continue to work in top gear. It seemed very low down on my list of priorities. Much more urgent was the ability and confidence to connect with anybody at all. It was not that all sexual feelings had gone: they simply had to be put on hold for a while, to allow me to function at a very basic level. To be expected to be sexual was just one more pressure no widow should feel obliged to respond to in her early fragile days. Sexual feeling does return in its own sweet time and sometimes, as I found out, at very unexpected times - often when one is touched by real kindness or humanity. I was never for a moment tempted to use sex as a way to finding comfort, escape or self-esteem, though there are a few women who go through a stage of bedhopping for precisely those reasons - often in the mistaken belief that it will magically help them create a new bond when in reality what often happens is that it acts as an anaesthetic and prevents them confronting the realities of their situation.

Sex, though, is often a bid to start a new relationship. There is tremendous social pressure to push one into another relationship again. This of course has ever been so, and it is reflected in the many proverbs that all more or less seem to indicate that unless you grab a widow fast and forcefully she is likely to become set in her ways and think twice about marrying again.

> 'Marry a widow before she leaves mourning.'
> George Herbert, *Jacula Prudentium*
> 'A good occasion of courtship is when the widow returns from the funeral.'
> 'He that woos a widow must take time by the forelock.'
> Thomas Delovery, *Jack of Newberry* circa 1597
> 'He'll have a lusty widow that will be woo'd and now wedded in a day.'
> Shakespeare, *The Taming of the Shrew*

Why all the haste? I wondered when I first read them. This particular brand of folk-wisdom seemed like distinct foolishness for someone who had just lost a partner; for we know that anyone who has been bereaved or suffered a loss could not possibly be ready for a new relationship until she has completely exorcized the old. However, my own experience of living through the first two and a half years of mourning showed me the truth at the heart of the folk-wisdom: namely that the widow is much more predisposed towards jumping into a new relationship very soon after her loss than after some time has elapsed, for the simple reason that her initial reaction to being alone is to replace the dead partner; and that if she then is forced to survive those early months and years alone she is likely to develop a uniquely individual spirit and perhaps rediscover the personality she may have never known in marriage where it so often lies buried. What I call 'finding the girl again' is a

process akin to what Carl Jung called individuation –
whereby the more mature person confronts those
conflicts and parts of the personality that have never
been lived out or given expression to, but have
somehow survived from adolescence and need to be
confronted once again. This is presumably why I and
so many like me find ourselves living out once again
some of the romantic dreams of our youth – and dating
the same types of men we rejected when we were
teenagers. But after a quick flurry of dating such men
about a year after Jacques died I opted for spending
Saturday nights alone with my cat watching Columbo
on television, or with one of the several safely platonic
male friends who were happy to sit in my kitchen and
eat my food. These latter friendships, interim friendships if you like, were a godsend – since I welcomed
and appreciated male company, but certainly at this
stage did not feel ready for a fully-fledged relationship.
I would recommend them to any widow as a way of
allowing her to feel feminine without the strings.

I became very aware of the pressure friends and
family applied to turn my thoughts in the direction of
marriage. 'Have you met anyone yet?' became a
familiar opening line to a telephone conversation – and
I'm not altogether convinced it is just your welfare the
enquirer has at heart. Yet finding an attachment, not to
say remarriage, after losing a partner is much more
problematical than people assume. It is not only that
statistically there are fewer men available after a
certain age, but simply because when one is thirty-five
plus and carrying a lot of luggage from the past
(including the habits of a lifetime) it requires an almost
superhuman effort to reconstruct an entirely new
social reality. In addition to this, of course, you have to

have the will to do so, and there are times, as I found out, when you simply lose all volition – either because you are tired, mentally or physically, or because the simple life begins to look increasingly preferable to the contortions and adjustments that would have to be made in a new partnership. Will he bring financial complications from an ex-wife? Will there be difficult teenagers? And if, at forty plus, he hasn't been married before, why not? There are so many questions you ask yourself.

I know there may come a time when I will be able to adjust to the complexities of life with step-children, for example, but in the first couple of years of bereavement I simply did not have the mental energy to invest in such relationships. I had first to learn to love my own company, before I could hope to reach out to others. I had first to regain confidence, to trust my ability to cope with life again. Step-children, ex-partners, business problems, problems of logistics – all could place considerable strain on a relationship at the best of times; and I was to find that most of the men available to the widow in her forties or fifties came with them all. In time I would learn perhaps to cope – but not while I was having virtually to relearn how to walk down the High Street. One step at a time.

I had always wondered why my own grandmother – extremely beautiful, widowed in her early thirties and left with five small children – had never remarried, especially in the light of her extreme religious orthodoxy, which almost demanded it. Now I think I understand. Once a woman is forced to cope alone she acquires, as I was to find out, a fierce independence which makes it increasingly difficult for her to take a man on board who would curtail some of that new-found freedom. A widow is in the unique position of being able to compare partnership with the single state, without the bitterness that so often accompanies divorce. After two years of making my own decisions, of eating whenever I liked, of taking up the whole of the double bed and watching whatever television programmes I fancied – after fighting all the daily battles with gas and electricity boards, with British Telecom and plumbers – I realized that I might now find it very hard to adjust to coupledom – especially since I had acquired a new confidence, a new awareness which would make it difficult for me to accept some of my former more submissive attitudes. Certainly coupledom did not look nearly as enticing at the end of two years as it did in the beginning.

The platitude that living alone makes one selfish does, of course, have much truth in it – especially now that living with a partner has become much more problematic for the working woman who, rather than being ready and available to do the supporting, comes home tired and herself in need of support. Like any twenty-two-year-old, when I first married I was altogether more malleable, more willing to please, than I am now. The times were different too: at that time marriage itself was considered a career. But in common with many women of my generation, I was caught between two stools – between the traditional values and expectations of the fifties, that marriage and family would take precedence over all else, and a burgeoning awareness through the growing women's movement of the sixties, that a woman had a duty to herself – indeed a right – to develop her own interests, career, or path.

I have come a long way from those early days, from

the years of putting myself through school again, to making those first tentative steps towards a career and financial independence. It had been a long-fought battle, and I was not willing to surrender my independence that easily. If I were to embark on a new partnership now, three decades later, it would quite simply have to be on my terms. Divorced women go through many of the same emotions – though they may come to it from a different vantage point. Widowhood offers some of the same learning processes and opportunities for self-discovery as divorce – but with some very definite differences. I must admit I have not found it particularly helpful to compare notes with divorcees, because often they are trying to eradicate hateful memories, and bring a bitterness and regret to the way they now view the opposite sex which I find very hard to reconcile with my own feelings. Many too have used a new relationship to precipitate them out of a bad marriage.

As a widow you gradually accept the reality of the loss of your partner – that he or she is physically not there for you in any shape or form. I remember lying on my side of the double bed at night with a huge toy panda on the side where Jacques used to sleep, and thinking that perhaps I could never again be special to anyone the way I had been to Jacques. It is an unexpected delight therefore, when, even momentarily, you find yourself the object of someone else's thoughts. To know that the *possibility of love exists* – that alone – can keep you going, for you forget how potent that feeling is. Almost the saddest thing about losing a partner is the feeling that with him you have lost all possibility of being loveable to anyone again: your loveability quotient plummets. The feeling of being loveless in that sense – of no longer being 'special' to someone is perhaps the bleakest of all. I have no doubt, too, that because of it one sends out all the wrong signals to men in the early days. This is the desperation that will send them scattering in the opposite direction. Alternatively, you may 'wish' yourself into a love-affair, create an unreal idealization that is doomed to disappointment. I was certainly not immune to this, as this diary extract shows:

> The temptation is to return to what one knew: the past is safe, the future such a threat and maybe there won't be one. Take men: when old flames phone it is tempting to remember what was, and hold onto the notion of a romantic past – dream of meeting again with renewed passion. After each telephone call from some man from the past who would somehow miraculously materialize (as much from curiosity on his part as mine) I'd spend a day day-dreaming, remembering the best moments of that relationship. It is so easy when you are on your own to kid yourself that you would be happy with anyone who would just show a little interest – a little tenderness, someone to invite round for a meal – and it is the easiest thing to fall back on someone you felt knew you very well at some point in your life, and convince yourself that he still knows you, still cares, and will understand.

Don't fool yourself. My best advice is, before you rush to invite him over, spend a little longer talking to him on the phone – and you may start to remember why you ended it all in the first place. You will probably find he will still be as over-weening, arrogant and blissfully insensitive to your feelings as he was all those years ago. He may even have become more so. Spend a little time interviewing him. The rule is that if he was inconsiderate, cold, and selfish then, now he will be ten times worse. Chances are, too, that any chemistry that may once have existed between you will no longer be there . . .

Many people use relationships as a way of avoiding mourning – as a distraction, even as an escape from their own feelings. I know one widow who was so terrified of being alone that she opted for the first man who came her way. He was patently unsuitable – younger, unstable, unemployed – but he soon moved into her big house where he proceeded to alienate all her friends as well as trying to spend all her money and taking over all her possessions. It was only several years later, when the young widow got herself a job, that she found the objectivity to see him as others saw him, and with her new-found self-respect was able to end the relationship. Better by far to risk loneliness for a while and find out that loneliness is actually bearable as it turns to self-discovery. If you do this you might find that your self-discovery takes you along some strange paths. You might find yourself moving through one type of man to another: for example in the early weeks or months, you might be attracted to someone for their sheer ebullience, or conversely, to someone for his tremendous sensitivity and quietness. It is probably what you need at the time with feelings so fragile: it is probably all you can handle. As the wound begins to heal, you find you can handle a wider range of emotions and personalities: that is another very good reason for waiting. You have to allow yourself to see what finally gels.

Those men who in the early days did not acknowledge my grief, or the intensity of my relationship with Jacques, were soon crossed off. How I longed for someone to know how I felt, for a man who could acknowledge my feelings, rather than the all-too-familiar male ready to jump on me in a vulnerable moment. How I longed for a nice kind man who would still accept me and even find me special and beautiful – and yet allow me my own sacred, hallowed past. I know I was asking the impossible in those painful early days. I felt like the wounded birds my children used to bring home who needed to be left in a cardboard box with cotton wool padding and fed and stroked from time to time until they healed.

When you do decide you might want a new relationship, where do you start? Single again, you come across the problem everyone in this position, divorced or bereaved, comes across: where do you meet an eligible man? In spite of what books might tell you, you are unlikely to bump into them in a supermarket, in the street, at airports, in pubs or on beaches (at least not after a certain age, if at all). Largely, you rely on invitations to gatherings where there might be the odd divorcee, bachelor or widower – and of course, you rely on people for invitations. That is why I always advise women to cultivate their women friends; generally speaking, however liberated, they still tend to make the social arrangements and do the inviting. Timing must be right: too soon and you retire battered and bruised – wait too long and you are no longer interested. There comes a time when you know you are ready to venture forth, and start a new relationship.

Solitude is preferable to forcing your feelings, spending time with someone you really do not wish to be with. I remember a positively ghastly evening I spent at the opera in the first year with the man I will call 'the Australian film director of little charm'. I love opera, it is one of my great passions, and one of my greatest joys is to share it with someone equally enthusiastic; but Lord knows how I had chosen the one escort who was bored from the first note of the first aria – so much so, that he started periodically to look at his watch. It was a hot evening and the opera house was not air-conditioned. The opera was Tchaikovsky's *Eugene Onegin*, which always depends on mood and subtle resonance. Yet all I was picking up were the vibes of 'what the hell am I doing here, when we could be in my hotel room?' I was irritated and reacted badly to my companion squirming about in his seat and yawning from time to time, as it was quite ruining the performance for me. Something in me snapped: in the interval I decided I had really had quite enough – and said, 'I'm sorry but I'm going home – I'm not enjoying this.' Leaving him quite speechless I leapt onto a bus to Paddington. I felt infinitely better when I arrived home, although I regretted missing the second half of the opera; and this taught me a valuable lesson. There is nothing wrong in valuing your own company to the extent that you would rather be on your own than settle for some boorish companion who is going to ruin your enjoyment anyway. I now spend perfectly contented hours at the opera, ballet and cinema completely alone, and much of the craving for a companion to share this with has disappeared.

I grossly misjudged my dates a couple of times. Often it was because of unrealistic expectations on both sides. I was seeing them as another Jacques, and they were seeing me as a desperate, needy woman. Once or twice it led to disaster and near violence. I seemed at times to suspend my usually good judgement – or perhaps I was simply out of practice. The most frightening instance happened one New Year's Eve, provoked by my wedding ring.

I had a real problem deciding what to do about the ring. I went on wearing it for quite some time because in my own mind I had not stopped being married. I would occasionally think that it was giving out the wrong signals – certainly to anyone who might be a potential partner – so on one or two occasions I decided to wear my ring on the other hand. I inevitably would feel very uncomfortable half an hour or so later, not least because the fingers on my right hand are fatter than those on my left, and the ring was tight. I would also start to feel amazingly guilty – worried that I might run into someone I knew whose eyes would immediately go to my naked left hand. I had a sensation of lightheadedess. I wondered if people would think that I was divorced. I would see people glance immediately at the left hand – and imagined them speculating about the white 'ring' of untanned flesh where the ring had been. It was a game I would play with myself which always ended up with me having to use suds to slide the ring back off the right hand and replacing it on the left. I realized I simply wasn't ready – nor perhaps would I ever be – to think of myself as 'unmarried' or 'decoupled'. On this occasion I was still wearing the ring.

Rather foolishly, I had invited someone I didn't

know very well, but who had seemed quite charming on the one or two occasions I had met him, to accompany me to the Chelsea Arts Club Ball. Jacques and I had always enjoyed it and though I was prepared for some nostalgia I was not at all prepared for the ferocity of this man's unprovoked attack. After a couple of drinks (and it was obviously this that provoked the ugly behaviour) he started to taunt me about the wedding ring I still wore – and sweating profusely after savagely whisking me round the dance floor in a tight clasp, he began to scream abuse at me. He then went to the bar where he spent the rest of the evening downing one drink after the other, tossing the occasional taunt in my direction – usually beginning with 'You ice-queen bitch'. I found myself sitting on a bench in the corridor weeping as everyone sang *Auld Lang Syne*, overcome by the combination of memories and his brutality. Because of the usual problem with transportation on New Year's Eve he had assured me that his own company driver would drive me back to my mother's house in North London, where I was to spend the night. Scarcely able to stand, reeking of alcohol, he staggered into the back seat, and remained sullenly silent throughout the journey while I was forced to keep up polite chit-chat with the driver who obviously knew nothing of what had occurred. Fighting back the tears I then had to face my mother (who had assumed I had had a jolly evening celebrating) without actually saying anything. I am sure she realized something was up, when I fled up the stairs trembling with barely a 'Goodnight'. I had not encountered the 'ugly drunk' for many years, and this came as such a shock and assault on my sensibility that I did not accept another date for six months.

One and a half years after Jacques' death I wrote:

It's hard – so hard. I become adolescent again
– like a vulnerable teenager. I fantasize about
patently unsuitable young men – and cry
when they let me down and stand me up. I
wait by the phone, hesitant to make the first
move. After all, my generation always waited
for the man to call. I realize I am sending out
all the wrong messages, am much too needy –
much too vulnerable.

Ideally what you are looking for in the early days is
companionship and warmth without any strings:
someone with whom you can share a laugh, or who
will make you feel protected. A good friend – a *chevalier*
rather than a lover.

I remember how shaky I felt on my first dates. I had
forgotten the *etiquette* of dating: I worried about
everything from what to wear, to what do I do if he
makes a move to kiss me in the car after dinner. Many
widows I have spoken to have expressed these same
fears: 'I'm not a young girl but I feel all the same
feelings again,' they say. 'I'm terrified of going on
dates.'

It is not only the fear of failure that causes many
widows to hold back from starting a new relationship
with a man. It is common for widows to feel that they
will in some way be disloyal to the memory of their late
husband if they do so. Feelings of guilt can be
compounded by insecurity and anxiety – the 'who
would ever fancy me at this age?' feeling, knowing that
it was fine to 'let it all hang out' with a partner who had
seen the waist-line gradually thicken over the years,

who was used to seeing you in all your morning un-glory; but how on earth could you ever get to that stage again? The problem is that your relationship was cut off at its most intimate stage and we have a natural tendency to want to start again where we left off: thus you want to skim through the lengthy and painful getting acquainted process, particularly with the fear of rejection lurking in your mind.

Apart from the 'who will ever fancy me?' fears there is also the 'who will I ever fancy?' factor: 'lust' at first sight undeniably becomes more problematic as you get older. The first time you are genuinely aroused by a man, you can feel a mixture of grief and relief – relief that part of you has not altogether died, that the juices still flow, and a tremendous sense of betraying your partner, greater than anything you could have felt in his lifetime. It was almost two years before I felt anything like desire for a man, and then it happened overwhelmingly, unexpectedly, out of the blue, and I wanted to sob with relief and overflow of feeling. It happened when I was away from home, which no doubt had lessened my anxieties and inhibitions. Nevertheless I spent the days tormented by guilt, much of which stemmed from earlier guilt unrelated to the present, but over which I had no control. Unsurprisingly the man looked like my husband, though strangely I only became aware of the resemblance afterwards. It was less physical than a certain quiet way of looking – a certain expression around the eyes – and when I saw it I grew doubly guilty. I dreamt about Jacques soon afterwards – a vivid sensual dream in which Jacques came to me and massaged the back of my neck. The re-awakening of my physical desires had brought back all the physical intensity of our own relationship. I am sure many widows experience this. I awoke from that dream in a semi-anaesthetized, drugged state, and felt very weepy. I craved physical contact with Jacques once again – and the yearning was almost more intense than anything I had experienced during my two years of bereavement. I walked around the house weeping. I thought that after two years I had got beyond that stage; but this hit me with renewed force. I think that I had managed to hide the passion of our relationship, especially in the early years, even from myself. I recently came across our early love-letters which so vividly recalled that passion, and once again I was taken by surprise. Was that me? Was that him?

One of the things I had been guilty of (and I am sure it has to do with the strategy of coping with bereavement) was in so burying myself in activity that I had not allowed these feelings to surface. Now on holiday in the sun in the company of someone who had re-awakened that part of myself, they all welled up and clamoured for my attention. In two years I had completely buried a part of myself – partly in memory of Jacques, partly because I simply had to get through the day and do tedious and demanding chores so that I could not even allow myself time to think love. It was a luxury, a distraction – a drain on my energy I did not need. I had not known if I would ever love again or not. Part of me said, yes, one of these days, when you are ready, it will come. I certainly had not gone out of my way to find it.

Even if you despair momentarily at the prospect of ever achieving another relationship, to believe in even the possibility of such a relationship happening in the future can sustain you. It is important to believe, and continually remind yourself, that you won't stay forever locked in grey bleakness and loneliness. Faith is the key, and perhaps one of the most important, and underrated, elements in mourning and recovery. By faith, I don't necessarily mean religious faith, but simply a faith in the power of life to renew itself and to heal. I count myself very fortunate in that I do have faith in the religious sense: that I believe in God and can pray to Him; but increasingly I find I can renew this faith in a number of ways. I often start the day by looking out of my bedroom window at a particular tree. It is an elderberry tree that has a nesting box that Jacques put there years ago – and a favourite place for all kinds of birds to congregate. The top of the tree is at eye-level and as I sit at my dressing table I can watch the little blue tits darting in and out, which I find very reassuring. It gives me faith in renewal – in continuity – and at the same time, a sense of the fragility of life.

I don't think you can over-estimate the part that faith plays in recovery from any loss, whether bereavement, loss of a limb or breast, or even redundancy: somehow you have to create the belief, the hope that there will be a better future. Though the leap into faith has to start from a change within your own heart, you can help this along by externals, whether in nature or the arts, whatever allows you to express certain emotions. There is nothing wrong with this. It is a rare person who can do it alone sitting staring at four blank walls, though when you read what human beings have been capable of, under the most adverse circumstances, you also become aware that faith can allow you to win through the most degrading experiences, as this often quoted passage from concentration camp survivor Victor Frankl expresses so forcefully:

What was really needed was a fundamental change in our attitude towards life. We had to learn ourselves and, furthermore, we had to teach the despairing men in the concentration camp that it did not really matter what we expected from life, but rather what life expected from us.

I am beginning to understand better what life expects from me.

Chapter Twelve

Unfinished Business

'Learn whence is sorrow and joy and love and hate, and waking though one would not, and sleeping though one would not, and falling in love though one would not. And if thou shouldst closely investigate these things, thou wilt find Him in thyself, one and many, just as the atom; thus finding from thyself a way out of thyself.'

Gnostic text

It is unlikely you will wake one morning and suddenly feel you are 'over it all'. Recovery takes as long as it takes; it may never happen completely but two years on I could write this:

Almost two years later I seem to have finally arrived at a sort of serenity – the closest I have ever got to it. There is a feeling of something altogether bigger and more important and enduring than the day-to-day hassles and trivialities as I sit in the autumnal garden looking at the trees heavily laden with fruit and the graceful golden rod. There is no doubt that the garden with its reflection of the seasons has helped: just looking at the weekly changes in the trees gives me a feeling of life's rhythms and patterns. I cannot then feel too worried about the ups and downs of everyday life. I try to stay as close to nature as possible via all my plants and animals. It

helps to have my ever-friendly black cat,
Deedee, there in the same place each day or
evening – waiting to be fed and stroked,
nagging to come in or out.

You know that you are on the road to recovery when
certain things begin to happen. A good indicator is
that your sleep patterns begin to return to normal and
that you can get a good night's sleep without that
awful four o'clock in the morning 'worry' period; when
you can face weekends and holidays without depression and when you wake up in the morning looking
forward to the day ahead; when you are less sensitive
to other people's often thoughtless comments. My real
test was being able to walk down the street lined with
chestnut trees where Jacques had taken his last
faltering evening steps. Every time I walked by the
trees on my way to the local shops I would think of
that – until there came a time when the trees were in
full flower, and I looked at them and just felt happy for
the miracle of the creamy waxen flowers. That took
three years.

My dreams had changed in character: they were
now telling me to change.

April 1990:

I was in a girl's dorm or some sort of dressing
room. There was lots of activity, girls dressing,
doing their hair, and talk of the big evening
event – a recital by Dustin Hoffman – in a
London theatre followed by dinner. It was *the*
glittering event that day in the capital. I had a
problem deciding what to wear: I pulled on

one item after another, ending up in a full
pink net shirt, a sort of maroon baseball jacket
over it – a strange combination. Part of my
hair (the pony tail) was pure white, the front,
a long fringe, was dyed blonde with the black
roots showing. I experimented putting it
back – then forward. It took me a long time.
All the others had gone. Suddenly I realized I
was on a boat going down a river towards the
sea. I frantically asked why I was here when I
was supposed to be in town. I was told there
were two events that evening: one, the
glittering theatrical one, the other a quiet
'nature' evening in the country – and I was
heading there. I told them there was a
mistake, and asked if I could be left off
somewhere: I was dropped on some seaside
front – where I hailed a bus back to London,
rushed into the theatre just as Hoffman was
finishing his performance, but still in time for
the dinner.

Arranging my hair was a major part of my dream –
this odd combination of white (old) blonde (trendy)
and fringe (young); as were the combination of clothes
– fancy, casual, short, glamorous, cute. I think this was a
dream about choices, telling me it was not too late to
turn around or change direction; also, about the
uncertain identity I was piecing together, bit by bit.

There are turning points throughout one's journey
through grief: each time you venture forth, 'feel the
fear and do it anyway' (in the words of an admirable
book), you are fortified. Two trips I made – to Russia
and to Israel – exemplified that feeling.

I was terrified of visiting Russia, alone, mid-winter, and still feeling so fragile. I had a million unvoiced fears: I worried about the food, the water, the language, official red-tape and the cold – yet at the same time I was in a state of immense excitement; for ever since I was thirteen, and had first read *War and Peace*, I had longed to return to my grandfather's birthplace. So when I finally received an official invitation to the first Leningrad Documentary Film Festival, just a year after Jacques' death, it seemed the right time to go – although I visualized Russia at that point as bleak and wintery as my own feelings at the time.

The two weeks I spent there turned out, in fact, to be two of the most enjoyable and intense weeks of my life – not only because I felt an immediate rapport with the people (it was the height of 'perestroika' fever), but because I did indeed feel a 'coming home'. And when I got back to England, I knew I had experienced something that had reached to the very depth of my being. It had also altered my perception – even the way I saw people in the streets, and in the local supermarket; for after the greyness and dinginess I had seen in Russia, everything here suddenly seemed a hundred times more colourful and abundant. I was at once aware of living a privileged life, where I could select from hundreds of different foods and other goods, yet at the same time I missed the warmth and generosity I experienced in Russia – a warmth and generosity that can only come from scarcity and deprivation. The effect on me was profound – and I am convinced it helped me come to terms with many unresolved aspects of my past.

*

I still needed to mourn my father, and it was my trip to Russia that helped me to do this; but I realized I had virtually put this aside and delayed it, partly because of all the other emotional overload, and partly because mourning a parent is, I think, quite a different process from mourning a partner. With the death of a spouse, one mourns the *future* or the loss of it, with a parent the past. With a partner, whatever the relationship, one has a definite time period to 'de-brief', and it is one that is quite recent: with a parent one has to go much further back, and that relationship may have been, as mine was because I saw my father infrequently in my early years, an incomplete one. In this sense, I think I had to mourn the relationship which I had so desperately denied, but which *wasn't* there first.

Although he had been born into an East European Hassidic family, he had, by virtue of necessity as a soldier, become much more liberal during the war years. My mother too, was not particularly religious, so it came as something of a surprise to everyone when my father decided to return to his Hassidic roots in the early fifties. My mother recalls that the worst rows at home were invariably over religion, and, as the first-born, I bore a lot of the brunt of this particular tension. Although emotionally drawn towards the more mystical side of Hassidism I started to question it very early on, making me a particularly infuriating daughter for my father, who at times was reduced to locking me in my room to make sure I didn't go out on the Sabbath Eve to see my favourite ballet or rehearse a school play!

He showed a marked ambivalence towards me. On the one hand he was proud of me, and yet so critical that a report card showing straight As in almost every subject except handwriting and PE would be greeted with 'And why the B+ for handwriting?' On the other, as his diaries show, he quite despaired of my growing independence of spirit and less than traditionally acquiescent nature. In common with many fathers he did not believe in praising me to my face, so that the communication we had was largely negative – whether it was comments on my hair or on my selfishness and disregard for others. I know that he boasted to his friends of my achievements, but I was rarely on the receiving end of his compliments or praise. Needless to say this did not work wonders for my self-esteem.

After he died, I tried desperately to remember moments of tenderness and intimacy we had shared. In the beginning, I could find very few such memories: instead I recalled the arguments, the shouting and the put-downs. In the immediate aftermath of his death I could remember very little that was positive or comforting; and this alone filled me with unutterable sadness. I could hear him telling me I looked like a 'witch' with my long hair, or shouting at me, as a sixteen-year-old, to remove 'that black' from around my eyes. I remembered his phrase: 'You don't count, it's other people that matter.' 'Why,' I cried to my mother the morning after he died, 'was I never daddy's little girl?' and I could find no consolation.

Today the memories are softer and I remember with affection the Sunday afternoon family outings when, dressed in baggy shorts like a scout master (even sometimes in winter) and with the hood of the car down, he would take us to Box Hill, Dorking, his favourite beauty spot, singing all the way. The car was a Singer, whose engine would often alarmingly catch fire: but still he would persist in calling it 'the best car on the road'. The alternative outing was to Southend-on-Sea, where we would visit the big funfair – the Kursaal – and walk along the promenade with candyfloss. On the way back through East London we would often stop off at Tubby Isaacs for fish and chips with masses of pickled onions and cucumbers – known by my father as 'wallies'.

I now know that like many people who appear easy-going he was actually a very shy man – that is, in personal relationships – although this was combined with a curiously uninhibited streak which would allow him to be the first to get up and dance with a belly-dancer in a nightclub, or whisk my mother on to the floor for a tango. He was also a very emotional man; but this emotion was just as likely to explode into frustration and anger as into affection. Now I better understand his shortcomings. In his last years he managed to complete a book – a sort of family history. 'All my children write,' he said, 'Why not me?' It took me three years before I could look at the typescript again – and now I treasure it for its quaint details, idealizations, even spelling and grammatical mistakes. I am better able to understand his struggles, wartime experiences and failures – many of which arose from his experience as a second generation immigrant. And I am at last able to recall some more tender moments we shared together, when he dropped his demands for a moment and became a gentle human being. I wish there had been more such moments – but which child doesn't?

When I light a memorial candle for my father each year, I no longer feel the sense of bruised rawness I felt at his sudden and untimely death, which had left me so shocked, that my right arm had immediately gone numb, and I thought I was having a heart attack too. I had sat through his Shiva knowing Jacques was ill and yet not quite cognisant of what was to come. The immediate effect of my father's death was to make me regress. I remember taking my toy panda to bed. I remember Jacques stroking my 'paralysed' hand again and again – even though he himself felt terrible. I remember trying to distract myself with my needle-point. I had to delay mourning until the right time appeared. Then I started to remember the better things.

Strangely, or perhaps logically enough, it was only when I made the trip to Leningrad that I really started to mourn him properly. Walking along Nevsky Prospekt or riding around Moscow, everything started to remind me of my father. I hadn't realized how Eastern European his whole personality and way of life was; it was only when confronted with food, for example, that seemed strangely familiar – the herrings, black bread and pickled cucumbers – that I started to dwell on this melange of cultures and customs he had bequeathed me. I remember sitting one morning in the auditorium of the Kirov Theatre watching the ballerina Natalia Makarova (who had returned under the auspices of the Festival to dance in her home town for the first time in nineteen years) rehearse. As I sat there relishing all the ornate splendour and the uniqueness of the historical moment, suddenly all my memories of my father came flooding back, and for the first time I felt I had grasped his very essence, and it was something I could only feel in Russia. It was as if I had to be in a remote place associated in some deep-rooted way with my childhood to allow myself to think these thoughts. It had a calming effect upon me; and from that time on, the memories were kinder.

*

The trip I made to Israel – the days spent at the seaside resort of Eilat, and then the family wedding I attended in Haifa – also had to do with identity, a need to touch base; and on a smaller scale, it also proved a healing step. A nephew of Jacques was marrying, and I was going to the wedding as representative of the Kupfermann family. My role of 'ambassador' was a new responsibility. I had become aware that as the family grew smaller and lost members those remaining had to take on additional tasks. Attending weddings abroad was one of them, as the family was far-flung, including branches in New York, Paris, Sydney and Zurich.

This diary extract shows the progress I had made:

> Two years and one month after Jacques' death, I sit gazing out over a shimmering oasis. Eilat is nothing but sand, sea and rock – with desert all around. The desert suits my mood – sparse, simple, arid, but clear and filled with light – the palm trees somehow symbolizing my own state: head buffeted by strong, cold desert winds (clean, dry winds through the mind), roots deep in the ground drinking in the water. Two years on and I can hold my head up high. I can take the strong winds. People remark on my new-found serenity. Few know how hard won it has been. It has followed a pattern – a period of anxiety, tension, agonizingly hard work followed by enforced relaxation, renewed self-examination and new ways of looking at problems.
>
> This was the first holiday where I had felt a

new easing of the heart. Even a gaiety (if I can use that lovely old-fashioned word) came over me. For the first time I had gone wanting to shed the burdens and heaviness of the past. A session with a counsellor had made me realize that I was at a cross-roads, with all kinds of major decisions to make regarding my work, the house, my children's futures – and I was somehow stuck in a mental impasse.

A week of calm and simple enjoyment in the desert was just what was needed to give me strength and resolution. I played table tennis and sunbathed by day, and ate and danced the Lambada by night with a gentle Texan businessman who had gallantly offered to be my 'walker'. The table tennis brought back some of my old girlish energy: although I hadn't picked up a bat in years, to my surprise, I could still play quite well – and springing around again attempting backhand smashes brought back some of the old spark. I can recommend a fairly undemanding game like this (but one that does require skill and energy) to anyone who feels they have lost their old 'attack'. It is amazing what a few wins at the ping-pong table can do!

Dancing the Lambada, with its sensual, even explicitly sexual movements, I started to feel the young girl coming back again, the girl who had jived, cha-cha'd and twisted all night. I had always loved dancing – and almost nothing for me was more frustrating than watching other people on the dance floor and having no partner. Now I was in the fortunate position of having a charming and present-able partner who loved dancing as much as I did: I was grateful to him for just that and no more – for making no demands I could not meet. I realized that I felt very different on this trip from any of the others I had taken in the past two years. I could even handle the airport (lugging cases had in the beginning been a bit of a nightmare and I had dreaded the long queues and ordeals of actually getting there), and felt less anxious flying. Something had happened to me; I had managed to jump some invisible hurdle.

So much of experiencing grief seems to involve going over old ground, exorcizing old ghosts, whether they consist of painful anniversaries or familiar journeys now done solo. Some widows make a point of deliberately going back to places they had shared and loved with their partners. I was one of these; it wasn't until I walked all the familiar paths on my own – from Cornwall to Woodstock, where we had spent the early years of our marriage – that I felt able to cope with the emotions these places conjured. Others often choose to avoid them, and while I am not sure that there is a 'right' solution, I know that for me, they had to be relived in order to be debriefed and emptied of all the fear and sadness they held – in order, in other words, that I could feel good about them again.

Fuchsia Cottage was very much Jacques. However, when I took a trip to Cornwall on what would have been our silver wedding anniversary, I was glad of company. These two diary extracts describe my feelings – both about long, lonely train journeys, and about the dreaded anniversary in the cottage.

It is on trains and airports that I feel most lonely – especially on the 'Cornish Riviera' taking me towards Bodmin Parkway. People on that train – often holiday-makers – are particularly friendly, and I always strike up conversations. I feel obliged to pour out my heart, to stop it lurching as the train pulls into the station, and the memory of all those summers comes flooding back.

I am very lucky with people on trains: I seem to attract the more interesting ones. (Jacques had always joked about that, claiming he always ended up opposite some po-faced civil servant buried in his newspaper.) On this occasion there were several MOD types travelling to Plymouth (where they all seemed to retire); a young mother with a ravishing baby like a Botticelli (the one thing that is guaranteed to cheer me up on a lonely trip is seeing a beautiful child, once again perhaps it reminds me of life, or even of the child within me), and a handsome young lieutenant in the Marines who came from the Isle of Mull. The young lieutenant promised to visit me in Cornwall and I was won by his unfailingly polite and pleasant manner.

Silver Wedding Anniversary (ours which would have been)

A date I had been dreading. The young lieutenant I had met on the train did come to Fuchsia Cottage as promised, all keen-eyed energy and surprisingly gentle and considerate. We walked over the rocks at Port Quin and I was quite touched when the six-foot-four-inch commando would not let me carry my handbag as I scrambled pathetically after him, he scaling the heights with no effort whatsoever. He fixed my rickety old front door lock too. I had had to leave it unlocked at night for fear of locking myself in. He hit upon the good idea of borrowing a rawlplug from next door, though heaven knows what they made of the tall blond young man who bounded up those stairs. At this point I didn't care: I was just so happy to have somebody with me on that particular day.

My childhood friend Jackie, who had been married the day before us and had just celebrated her silver wedding anniversary, had sent a beautiful bouquet of flowers to the cottage. I arranged them in my favourite cobalt blue jug (they were various shades of pink) and I just kept looking at them on my pine dresser. I didn't feel as sad as I looked, for with preparations for a visitor, I was almost excited. I felt I was doing something positive for a change.

Learning to reconstruct your own social reality anew means learning to perceive things through your own eyes afresh. I cannot speak for women married to men in other professions or jobs, but I became acutely aware after Jacques died how involved I had been in the role of artist's wife: how much his perceptions – especially visual ones – had influenced my own. Living with an artist for so many years to some extent affected the way I saw the seasons, as is apparent from this diary extract:

The sadness changes with every season: as a painter's wife for much of my life I had grown to see the changing landscape through his eyes and his paintings: autumn particularly reminds me of him: paintings of the browns, reds, golds of the trees – those trees which were so much a symbol to him. Even the skies became Kupfermann skies. He taught me to look at light and shadow, clouds and rays of sunlight with a new eye. How can I look at those trees and clouds and not think of him – especially this year, with the extraordinary Indian summer which made the reds and yellows so sharp, rather like the New England fall? We are not aware how during marriage, so much of our vision is influenced by our partner – especially when he is an artist with a particularly strong vision of the world. After two years I still see the world through his eyes – but I am starting to do my own paintings, so perhaps I will produce my own vision.

This was hardly surprising, since for all the years we had been together, Jacques had lived, breathed and even 'slept' his painting. The air of the house was filled with the smell of turpentine and freshly squeezed oil paints: there were often trails of paint up the stairs, canvases propped up temporarily against tables or chairs, easels hauled up and down stairs. To this day I can still hear him treading on the squeaky floorboards in his studio, where he would sit for hours, squinting at a near blank canvas: where the children would always knock first to ask if they might come in, fearful of disturbing an almost ferocious concentration. Jacques would bring that same concentration down to dinner, and he would often bring the painting down too, place it in front of him, and sit staring at it throughout the meal – especially if he had reached some sort of 'impasse'.

Artists' wives learn to live with the 'mistress' – a much deadlier, more intransigent rival than any other woman could be. Sometimes Jacques would not speak for days, not because he was being moody but simply because he was so wrapped up in a painting: he simply didn't want to lose concentration. This was not always easy for me as I am a garrulous creature by nature, but I learned eventually to accommodate it. Perhaps my own writing and research was partly a way of dealing with Jacques' intense shutting out of the world. I know that I sometimes resented it, but I know, too, that I deeply admired and even envied his ability to concentrate in this way. When a painting was finished he would always ask me to criticize it honestly and a dialogue would begin.

I hadn't been aware of how imperceptibly over the years I had absorbed many of his perceptions, especially regarding landscape and skies. This, of course, is part of the social construction of the reality a couple build together, and is not easily de-constructed. Jacques' vision, in other words, will probably stay with me for many years to come.

Learning to have your own vision means neutralizing all the places, objects, events that you perceived jointly – learning to connect with the world in new ways, going over all the old routes and re-learning them. First it is necessary to go back and see them again *as you both saw them* before they can take on your own personal separate meaning.

It took me four years to start to see things through my own eyes, and I have begun at last to do my own painting again. Jacques had always encouraged me above all to draw, telling me that I had a good line, and that it was mainly a question of *looking*. I now know that this is something I would like to develop, that the very act of painting opens new channels of expression in me, and allows me to connect to the world in ways I have been incapable of doing for a long time.

Chapter Thirteen

Completing the Circle

'As I have discovered passionate grief does not link us with the dead but cuts us off from them.'

C. S. Lewis, *A Grief Observed*, 1961

I had difficulty understanding this thought at first, but now I know exactly what Lewis meant: it is only when you have rediscovered some equilibrium – some way of feeling part of the world or of being linked to life again – that you accept the continuing presence of the loved one. I know, for example, that I do not feel Jacques' presence when I am bitter, angry or upset: on the contrary, I never feel more alone than at these times. It is only when I am happily enjoying something that I feel a sense of continuity and oneness: that there has been no break – no loss. It is when you experience this feeling, too, that you know healing has taken place.

Many widows feel frustrated that they cannot picture their husband's face precisely when they want to, especially in the early days. For the first year or so after Jacques' death I blocked out picturing him at all (except in dreams) since my last memories of him had been as a wasted shell of the man I had known – and I did not wish to recall those nightmare visions. Now I finally can conjure up the man I knew before the illness struck, and I can do so with serenity and calm. I can even smile at some of his foibles: the way he resolutely refused to have some crooked teeth straightened, or the way he fussed over one or two thinner spots in his otherwise luxuriant mop of white hair. As he grew older and the features refined, he lost his 'Bogey' look, and he looked more like the late cellist Paul Tortelier. I actually watched a television masterclass by Tortelier recently and almost felt Jacques' presence through their uncanny resemblance.

Recovery means you feel the continuity in so many different things. Some have called this 'absorbing' the dead person. There comes a point where you realize (and perhaps this is the point at which you gain some measure of serenity) that the person you have lost lives on – in you, your children and in the world at large. This serenity can appear in the midst of apparent chaos. The first time this struck me forcefully was in the first week of September 1989. I had had a very trying week of coping with all the usual household frustrations, bills, repairs, children's problems and an extra heavy work-load. I had heard too, that the friend who had been struggling with cancer had rapidly deteriorated and had gone in to a hospice. My heart was particularly heavy. It had been a long and unusually hot summer, with little rain. My pride and joy had been successfully growing a sunflower – just one. Though I had started with a whole row, the aphids had been merciless and left me with just the one, which grew at the rate of Jack's beanstalk. To me, it was magical: it was like the eyes of a portrait that followed you everywhere. I could see it both from my bedroom window and from the kitchen window, and it opened up into a radiant golden shaggy head. As it had grown I had talked to it, coaxed and cajoled it. I could understand why man had worshipped streams, trees and stones. I praised it every day for its brilliant beauty: for me, it was a sign of God – that He was in my garden, giving me hope and faith in the future.

Then that day in September something told me I must capture the sunflower on paper – I must draw or paint it. I hadn't painted in years: it had needed all Jacques' encouragement in the past to make me do it – and when he had gone, I had let that side of myself go too. Now I knew the time was ripe for me to cultivate it again, and I sat in the garden sketching my sunflower. The first lines were shaky, but gradually my confidence returned, the line got steadier, and the resulting painting pleased me no end. It had given me the feeling that Jacques was somehow living on in me – telling me to use that part of myself – and it made me very happy. I know now that this is a natural stage of mourning, that we must integrate the dead person, absorb him or her, into ourselves.

Everyone does it in different ways. With my mother, it was gardening. My father had always been a very keen gardener: but not so my mother. The house was her domain. After a year or so of entirely neglecting the lawns and flower beds, she suddenly called me one day and said 'Guess what? I've started to do the garden.' She had acquired a new electric mower and some tools, and with the help of her gentleman friend she was starting to engage in an activity which was entirely new and alien to her. I noticed it corresponded to one of the anniversaries of my father's death. Thus we find widows taking on the most extraordinary roles – from businesses to mountaineering. I know one widow whose husband had been a great outdoor type while she had always been happier staying home with a book who, a year after her husband's death, took herself off on a walking tour of the Lake District and then started a course in mountaineering – at the age of fifty-three.

For some, 'absorbing' is a half-way measure. They may only take on the new-found activity or interest for a brief period until they find something they want to do more. They may eventually sell the shop or business they struggled with so gamely or, as in my mother's case, engage an occasional gardener to take over; but in any case 'absorption' signals recovery – a sign that the death has made its way into the flow of life again.

Looking back over the past few years I see that I moved in fits and starts largely because of my resistance to change. I could not change until I had wrung every last bit of meaning out of my past, out of the events which led to the person I had become. This is why, I suppose, some people embark on psycho-analysis. A sudden bereavement has many of the same effects as when you are forced to de-brief a marriage or a relationship, except the only guide you have to lead you through the labyrinth of your own past, is yourself. During the early years of mourning you are so often flooded with the 'where has it all gone' feeling that the only way to find out may be to return to the very memories that produce it. This extract describes that feeling:

> Even after more than three years the discovery of an old photograph or document relating to Jacques can bring back all the old sadness. My children are acutely aware of this. I came in one day to find them whispering conspira-torially. They beat a hasty retreat up the stairs and I was aware that they were trying to hide

something from me. That something was Jacques' faded demob papers and a picture of us taken on our honeymoon, crossing the Atlantic on the *Queen Mary*. Elias had found a box full of old papers and photographs, damp and mouldering in the cellar, and was attempting to dry them out and restore them. He had kept them from me, he said for fear of upsetting me. When I saw the yellowed paper and the picture of the young couple at the dining table – Jacques with a head of black hair and I with piled-up sixties hair looking, I am sure I had hoped, not unlike my idol of the time, Audrey Hepburn, terrible loneliness swept over me, and I quickly put the photos and papers away in a drawer. It was just too painful for me to look, even though so much time had elapsed. 'Where had it all gone?'

Death forces you to look at these frozen frames of the past and continually ask that question. I tend to panic when my memory fails me and I cannot entirely remember the details of the scene. You imagine you will remember everything with crystal-clear clarity forever – and the truth is, you don't. Who, for example, were this rather disagreeable looking, frumpish, middle-aged couple sitting with us at the table on the *Queen Mary*? Where did I get that dress I was wearing and what colour was it? This was after all our honeymoon voyage; but all I recall was that we had splashed out on cabin class as opposed to economy tickets, and as luck had it they had overbooked this class and were forced to accommodate us in first class, with the luxury of a suite of rooms, real beds and breakfast wheeled in on a vast trolley with all kinds of marvellous dishes in huge silver tureens.

I remember, too, from that voyage, that Jacques had been deeply immersed in a book I had just given him: Gunther Grass's *The Tin Drum*. When he read a book his concentration was total. I have vague memories even today of wanting him to put down *The Tin Drum* and talk to me instead; of feelings of insecurity and fear for what lay ahead for this twenty-two-year-old bride on a strange continent with a man who was practically a stranger . . . Perhaps this was the loneliness I felt as I looked at the photograph. This longing to put the clock back and relive those moments all over again may fade a little with time, but it never altogether goes away.

We all tend to idealize the dead, especially in the first shock of bereavement. Some however, never get beyond that idealization, which often masks a welter of ambiguous feelings, guilt and even resentment. In many ways it is safer to idealize: that way, you never have to own up to the negative feelings that are part and parcel of any relationship. It is particularly difficult not to idealize when that person has ended his life in great pain and suffering and fought a heroic battle. The 'why' of suffering quite obliterates everything else. 'He fought to the end' was one of the inscriptions I put on Jacques' tombstone, for it was that fight at the time that seemed to sum the man up.

It took me at least two years to allow myself to talk

about some of Jacques' more human failings: to look at him as an ordinary man – in spite of the fact that some aspects of his life, his talent, and his ending, had been so far from ordinary. The sheer shock of his death and especially the feeling that he had been cut down, so unfairly robbed of life, quite eclipsed all other feelings for a long time. It had also made me idealize our entire relationship, though the truth was, like all long-term relationships, it had been through some rocky patches. Some related to the financial problems which go with 'the starving profession', though in the later years Jacques had started to do well professionally; some to my earlier illness, which had created havoc in the household; and yet others to the contradictions inherent in the very condition of being an artist who wanted both freedom to create, and yet somehow had to keep the money coming in to pay the bills. 'Artists shouldn't marry,' he would sometimes say; and yet I knew that he placed a very high premium on home, family and security.

Above all though, Jacques had always had a certain sadness hanging over him. It had been there right from the beginning, even before we had married, and I knew it stemmed from the loss of his own family in the Holocaust – his own impotence at having been unable to rescue them, about which he had always been very reluctant to talk. I sensed that he had buried this grief at his lost childhood, deep within himself. I know that Jacques guarded his secret grief and had built up tremendous defences – painting, to some extent, had been his way out of this hell; but there was still much there that he had never come to terms with and that he was unwilling to communicate in words. This had sometimes caused problems in communication between not only ourselves, but between him and the children too. He would sometimes spend whole days in silence. Jacques, I now know, had never done his own 'grief work'. The sad thing is that only now, through my own grief, can I understand it: the long silences, the cutting off (at times he would seem to be almost in a trance – even in a room full of people), the total immersion in his work, the deeply etched lines on his face – this was all part of the silent sadness he had carried around with him from his childhood, and which I can now understand: then I could not. There must be many like him, not only Holocaust survivors but victims of other tragedies, who carry around this silent burden of grief. It has taken my own mourning to understand this. We are all to some extent survivors of loss: the loss of our childhood, of a hope, a dream – as well as the loss of a loved one through death. We live with so much fear and silence surrounding loss, sometimes greatly inhibiting our ability to live fully and courageously in the present. Yet how do you begin to reach this most deeply defended and vulnerable area, especially when the expression of sadness at loss is culturally discouraged?

It was only when I began to see the man as a real person with all his flaws, when I stopped idealizing him, that going to Vienna became a compulsion – the only way I could complete the circle.

I now know that much of my restless behaviour over the past three and a half years has been a sort of primitive searching for my lost partner – that everything from the endless pacing about the kitchen mopping surfaces to my trips abroad – can be understood within the framework of the 'pangs' of grief which precipitate what Colin Murray Parkes, in his book *Bereavement,* has called 'anxious pining'. This, I learned, was the emotional component of an urge to search for a lost object which all human beings share, in common with the greylag goose. I must admit it is almost reassuring to know this.

I knew there was one last place I might find him – or at least find the 'him' I hadn't quite understood. I had one last task to complete before I could call my 'grief work' finished. It was a task I was completing on behalf of Jacques almost: and it was to go to Vienna, and finally confront the city that had both formed him and brought him so much suffering. I had wanted to go earlier but could not bring myself to do so. First I had to reach the point where I could not only see Jacques as a real person but somehow 'crack' his deeply hidden, inner kernel, the key to the heaviness, the sorrow that he carried around with him which showed in his slightly stooped posture. I knew that it in some way related to his birthplace, to the sadness of a lost childhood – a childhood sabotaged, a family destroyed by the Nazi occupation of Vienna.

In all his conversations with me Jacques had made it clear that he had never forgotten Vienna. Not only did he remember the privations and the interrupted schooling of those years, and the occasional beatings up he received on the streets from gangs of Hitler Youth; but most traumatic of all, he remembered having to leave on one of the last of the children's trains in 1940 and make his own way to Holland (which was just about to be occupied too) and then to America. There he had only very distant family and he suffered not only the loneliness that every refugee experiences, but the terrible helplessness of the child who had tried desperately, but in vain, to persuade those relatives to find the money that he thought it needed to get his parents out. For the rest of his life he was to carry around the last tragic letter he had received from his parents begging him, a child of twelve, to try and find the money to rescue them. We shall never know if there was any real possibility of that solution; but his inability to find the money was to leave him with the guilt not only of the survivor who had outlived his family, but of a son who had failed.

His father had been a self-taught lawyer and inventor; his mother, a governess to a minor member of the Austrian royal family. He had been brought up with books, poetry and a love for art and beauty. His American relatives were not at all from the same kind of cultured background or class: he saw them as philistines who treated him like a second-class citizen and another unwelcome mouth to feed. Worst of all they had little respect or understanding for his artistic talents and ambition and cut him off entirely from the world of Goethe and Schiller he had grown up with. For much as he was later to detest it, Jacques was very much a product of the Vienna of that time, which, prior to the *Anschluss*, had been a glittering hot-bed of intellectual and artistic activity.

At the end of the war he returned briefly to Vienna to try to trace his parents. On returning to his childhood home he found that neighbours had denounced them and they had been deported; though he only discovered where – the name of the concentration camp – through a legal search in the nineteen-eighties. His first instinct on learning the news was, he admitted, 'to go out and kill as many Nazis as he could find'. This, he never did, of course, but some of that instinct and anger stayed with him. It exhibited itself above all in his dislike for the treacly charm of the Viennese.

Apart from that traumatic visit, he was never to return to Vienna, and all his life spoke about the vicious anti-semitic streak in the typical lower-middle-class Viennese. He had no desire, he said, to see the beautiful buildings or listen to the Vienna Boys Choir. He knew what lay beneath it. By the same token he refused to speak German, though he did occasionally write it to the few German-speaking relatives still living in Switzerland.

Later on, he was in fact to be reconciled to Germany, painting the portrait of the head of one of the major breweries – but never to Austria. Yet all the time I had known him, he had also betrayed his Viennese upbringing – not only in his love for Beethoven and Goethe but in his craving for certain foods: plum dumplings, anything with pastry and apple, every-thing fried and swimming in butter – and cream and jam with everything. He had talked too of the Vienna Woods where he had first learned to love nature, the amusement park (the Prater), the school he attended, and his frequent visits to the Natural History Museum (as a young boy he had wanted to be a naturalist).

I was sorry we had never made a trip to Vienna together to confront his past. When, after his death, I discovered the little battered album of wartime photographs from Vienna that he had carried around with him everywhere, with pictures of the street where he had lived, the Big Wheel of the Prater, St Stephen's Cathedral and other landmarks, I could almost feel the young boy and his search at the end of the war, and I knew that I would never exorcize

Jacques' pain over his lost childhood and family until I
visited Vienna and came face to face with these ghosts.
All Jews carry this double burden of mourning. We are
born grieving – mourning six million from the recent
past. This would be the very last stage of my own
mourning; I knew that once I had done it I could
somehow put it behind me and get on with life, as is
specified in the Jewish religion itself.

In my heart of hearts I was dreading the trip, but I
found all kinds of other reasons why I ought to go. It
was the Mozart Bicentenary Year; I thought this
sugared the pill somewhat, and I tried to look forward
to attending a concert or two, visiting Mozart's house
and the hunting lodge at Mayerling. But I knew my
real task, the real purpose of my visit, was something
else.

As the day approached for the trip, I felt myself
overcome by terror. I had suffered a panic attack –
shortness of breath and dizziness – while out
shopping the day before. I was warned that I might
have a similar attack, either on the plane (and I don't
look forward to flying at the best of times) or in Vienna
itself. What would I do in a strange city if I started to
feel faint and weak at the knees? I had booked myself
into a small but comfortable hotel, the Beethoven,
right in the centre, and I knew exactly what I had to do:
find the street where Jacques had lived as a child and
walk along it; take a ride in the Vienna Woods; visit the
Prater and ride on the Big Wheel; visit some of the
other landmarks in his photographs.

It was strange travelling with a planeload of people
who had other, more innocent agendas – who were
there simply to have a good time, to enjoy the
splendours of the Imperial City; to go to concerts, eat,

drink and be merry in the Grinzig. How could they possibly know the emotional load I carried, or the purpose of my own trip? I tried politely to explain to a few friendly fellow passengers who enquired, that it was a 'sentimental journey', though it was far from sentimental in the romantic sense usually implied. There was little loving nostalgia: rather I was carrying unresolved bitterness and hatred. How could I explain these feelings? – that for me, going to Vienna was like stepping back into the past and meeting the Nazis face to face: that I was preparing not to love but to hate the city?

There was heavy cloud as we landed, and the Danube looked a dirty greyish-brown – which did not displease me, as this was entirely in keeping with my mood. After checking into the hotel, I crossed the road to get something to eat at a typical Viennese cafe which was full of slightly seedy types buried behind vast newspapers on rollers. I ordered an omelette, thinking I needed sustenance for the task ahead. I then took a taxi to the Sixth District and Erdebergstrasse, the street where Jacques had lived. I only had the old photographs taken in 1945, to go by, and much of it had obviously been rebuilt. It started to rain and was getting dark fast. I put up my umbrella and walked the entire length of the street, closely examining every doorway and the façade of every old building that still stood, to see if I could identify the house. It was like walking back in time, and for a second or two I experienced real panic: my knees gave way and my heart started to pound.

What was I expecting to see? Jacques' ghost appear in a doorway somewhere? I don't really know; yet I do know I had to absorb the atmosphere of that street – to walk the same pavements he had walked as a young boy. Although the shops and cafes had undoubtedly changed there were still a few old enclaves that I recognized from the photographs. I carefully snapped them all and suddenly came to a very old building which turned out to be the District Infants School. This had to be the one Jacques had attended, so I decided to go inside. I had the strangest feeling as I pushed open the heavy wooden and iron door and stood in the shabby entrance hall where children still loitered: I had such a strong sense of the presence of that lost child.

I had the same feeling the next day standing in the cavernous entrance way to the vast Natural History Museum where I briefly glimpsed the fossils and reconstructed dinosaurs that Jacques must have looked at as a child. The Vienna that I visited was a very different one from that enjoyed by the other tourists on my charter flight, who raved about the splendours of the Schönbrun Palace or the Belvedere. I too took in the baroque magnificence of the Opera House, the theatres, concert halls and palaces: I too ate chocolate cake at Sachers, visited Mayerling – a rather gloomy and disappointing place. But when I rode on the Ferris Wheel at the Prater I was thinking less of the view than of the child who used to go there for a treat at weekends in the thirties.

At a superficial level, I could enjoy the art, the music and the rococo charm of the buildings – and especially the hospitality of a dashing young Viennese conductor whom I met after a concert given by the Oxford Orchestra, and who invited me to see a play of Goethe's at the National Theatre, and wined, dined and whirled me round the old city at night. But at a profound level, I hated it; I found the whole place heavy, lugubrious, unnaturally quiet, like a museum, living in the past; even the young people looked old and lacked spontaneity. It reminded me of parts of German Switzerland. It struck me that the ordinary people I met serving in the shops or restaurants exhibited exactly the same dourness and pettiness that Jacques had always described to me. I don't think I was just carrying over his feelings from the past, for I saw several demonstrations of this kind of meanness, especially if I tried to act in a non-regulated or spontaneous manner – whether it was asking for something that was off a menu, or not crossing the road at the right time.

Personally I saw little evidence of the famous Viennese charm. On the contrary sullen stares and outright rudeness seemed to be the general way of behaving – and a certain resentment towards all non-German speaking people. I asked a friendly German professor of psychiatry I had met at the theatre to try and explain the feeling of heaviness I got about the city. He told me that the Viennese are 'a mixture of the cultured and the materialistic – not the idealistic – and that to understand them one has to spend a few hours at one of their grandiose Catholic cemeteries'. He summed up the city in one word, 'necrophiliac'. 'Do you understand that?' he asked over a drink in the interval. I most certainly did – but I had mistakenly thought it was because I was identifying this with all of Jacques' experiences and that perhaps other people did not feel it. He explained it as a result of a mixture of the history of the city, the Catholic Church and the particular mix of 'Tribes' who live there.

One certainly notices the 'Tribes' as he called them:

the fierce stares of the Hungarians, the shabby Yugoslav peddlers, and the surprisingly beautiful and chic young Russians I had met on the underground. One could feel all the old nationalisms virtually boiling over at this particular time, for as Eastern Europe fast collapses and suffers civil war, Vienna is full of desperate people either trying to make a living or escape from the turbulence.

The German professor looked surprisingly like Jacques in profile – the same fine features and thick white hair. Looking at him I found it hard to hold back the tears. I had cried three times in Vienna: once, when I had walked into the Infants' School in Erdeberg-strasse; again, when I had ridden through the Vienna Woods dappled green and gold, just like one of Jacques' paintings. I had suddenly realized that this was where it had all started, and I thought again of *Maytime*, the first and last film Jacques had ever seen, with those scenes of Jeanette MacDonald riding in a carriage through the woods – the scene which provided almost the opening and the closing frame of Jacques' life. Then I cried again, a third time, looking at this kind stranger in the theatre – who was telling me that Vienna was a city of death.

Waiting in the hotel lobby for the taxi to take me to the airport, I reflected that I had, at long last, exorcized Vienna. Something had compelled me to get to the heart of Jacques' darkness, to know and to understand the great weight he had carried around – the weight that had bent his very back and ultimately, I can't help but feel, contributed to his early demise. Now I think I understand. I was glad to leave those monumental and oppressive buildings.

It was cloudy when we touched down at Gatwick,

but the air felt fresher, and less stifling. I noticed the leaves had practically all fallen in my absence and most of the flowers in my garden had finally gone. For two days afterwards, I could scarcely speak; I felt a terrible tiredness and inertia. After most trips I normally felt elated: this time, I only felt a weariness. I telephoned no one – but I knew my mission had been accomplished. Vienna had been an 'impasse'. I now know too that Jacques' inability to come to terms with the city that he felt had destroyed so much of his life had also become something of a block between us. This secret sadness which I could not penetrate (and this impasse had often made me feel frustrated, guilty and helpless) had led to quarrels which were avoiding the central issue, his big secret as it were. Faced with long impenetrable silences I would ask again and again, 'What is it?' 'What can't you tell me?'; but how could he tell me about Vienna? I was left to find out for myself. I now understand a little better where Jacques had come from, what he had left behind and what he had brought with him.

Many widows, I am sure, work on 'unfinished business' after their husbands die; in some cases, it involves righting quarrels within the family or with business partners; in others, like mine, it means making a physical journey which symbolizes something else. Some re-live their honeymoon or some particularly wonderful holiday. I had to re-live this trip to Vienna. I had to make 'his' journey and feel again the disturbing echoes of a very dark past. I am glad I have done it: re-experienced his pain and anger. It has freed me to go on.

The day after my return I fell into a deep sleep in the afternoon – a sleep that seemed to wash away much of the anguish and anxiety I had been feeling over the last week. I woke up sensing my mood had changed: I felt as if a great weight had been lifted. The next day the weather turned crisp and cold, the leaves were falling fast. I walked along the familiar avenue of chestnut trees where Jacques sang his haunting song, and looked at the ground covered in shiny chestnuts. Suddenly I felt as free as the child who used to collect conkers to put on a string and play with her brothers. Discovering the lost child in Jacques had somehow released that part of myself too.

Epilogue

Invincible Summer

'There was a roaring in the wind all night;
The rain came heavily and fell in floods;
But now the sun is rising, calm and bright.'

William Wordsworth

You are almost at the end of your journey, but how do you know when you have succeeded in completing 'grief work'? Progress comes not smoothly but in fits and starts, and only you can know when you have made it: there will be certain 'landmarks' or key events which take on a special significance. You can instantly sense when you have crossed certain thresholds, indicating that you have somehow found the courage to move on: that a new identity is slowly but surely emerging.

Take this one seemingly trivial example. April 1991 was the first time I had ever entered a betting shop to place my own bet (though I had often had a little flutter in the past on the Derby and the Grand National). I felt like someone entering a saloon bar in the Wild West as I fought my way through the fudge of heavy smoke and rows of seedy-looking regulars. I knew that Jacques would have been proud of me. I hadn't a clue what to do – only that I had an urge to put some money on both Bonanza Boy and Bigsun in the Grand National. I had no idea how to fill in a form and ended up asking some old punter with a pock-marked nose and a handful of flashy rings to help me. He persuaded me to back two other horses as well, and I ended up spending a small fortune and winning a pound. I wasn't exactly thrilled but I knew that for me this had been some kind of coming-of-age. Everyone has to find their own significant landmarks. Recognizing them is half the battle.

You are absolutely aware when the 'ghosts' depart. With me something definitely happened in the winter of 1991, between the months of November and February. A combination of a grim economic climate, freezing cold weather, debilitating bouts of 'flu and the fourth anniversary of Jacques' death hovering over me as always made these months difficult, and I was all set to go into a seasonal decline. There were a few shaky days over Christmas; but on recovering my balance, I felt a subtle difference from the way I had felt before. I no longer thought I heard Jacques treading on creaky boards in the studio: the only sound now was the hum of Elias' micro-fiche reader. I used one of Jacques' old watercolour paint boxes and brushes for a small study of some Christmas roses which I gave away as a gift and felt good that they were actually being used again. I now feel able to move the old wardrobe in the studio where I kept the last remnants of Jacques' clothes. The roll-top desk which housed a toppling mound of his old sketch-pads, photos and papers, will be stripped and refinished.

For much of the past four years I have been standing still. I have spent so much of my time simply looking: watching the birds from my window, or the plants in my garden, or passers-by in the High Street. Jacques used to tell me that you could learn everything you had to know from looking. I am beginning to understand what he meant.

I have spent much of my time, too, building

breakwaters against the rough seas. E. M. Forster wrote: 'We are all of us bubbles on an extremely rough sea. Into this sea humanity has built as it were some little breakwaters - scientific knowledge, civilized restraint - so that the bubbles do not break so frequently or so soon. But the sea has not altered.' I know that my home, my garden, my white room with the books and paintings, the Cornish clifftops and all the other familiar places have served as my 'breakwaters' over the past four years. But I know now I can risk going further afield, and regularly scour the property sections of the newspapers for a pretty house abroad. I am not even sure *where* it will be but I have images of the south - blue skies and bougainvillea - that correspond to the 'summer' breaking through.

I am not convinced that I have completely finished my 'grief work', but much has been accomplished. I know there are still some shadowy areas of my past that I have yet to summon the courage to look at in the full light of day, but at least I am aware of the shadows and have resolved one day, perhaps with the support of a loved one, to exorcize these too.

I am beginning at last to feel love beckoning. For a long time it has been almost like a personal tug of war: the past and its ghosts pull one way, with the occasional weaker tug from the future. Love, of course, represents a great leap into the unknown: taking risks again - above all, risking loss. I know now I *can* take that risk and survive intact.

In those four years I have swung back and forth as far as my feelings about a new partnership go. After two and a half years, I wrote:

The urgency of 'feeling special' to someone has gone. I have come to feel that it is more important to feel special to myself – that my identity, loveability and happiness do not depend on another – which does not mean I do not on occasion crave the company of someone with whom to share all my intimate moments, my sorrows as well as my joys, but I know now it does not necessarily have to be one person. I had had that person: he found me at a time in my life when I had not yet discovered what my likes and dislikes, joys and sorrows were; we discovered them together and in some ways he moulded them. Now it will be very different; I know the corners of the earth that I love; the flowers, scents and sounds that delight me. It is not that life is no longer a discovery but rather that the topography is no longer totally unfamiliar. Now I cherish the old rather than the new. There is no longer one person who can share the sunset at Sounion with me; or rather there is, myself. I am alone, but not lonely, because I have taken into me every-thing I ever shared with Jacques.

Today, however, I feel somewhat differently again: I know that I *can* exist quite happily without a partner, but I know too, that certain parts of myself will never be given expression if I do. Thus I could write recently:

Although I am approaching fifty I am not yet old enough to renounce the idea of love. We can exist without love but, alone, we will

never be put to the test, never be asked to
grow in a certain way, never be stretched to
the full. I am willing to pay the price for a love
that brings out my hidden strengths, for
without it, I feel I will live a diminished
existence, however problem-free.

I know I have changed physically too. Catching a
glimpse of myself in a mirror in Cornwall in February
1990 I wrote:

My face has changed. The contours may be
the same, the smile the same, and I am still
relatively unlined, but I see a new expression,
and I am not sure if I like it or not. I see the
look of a wounded animal, but its ferocity also
startles me. It looks like some Asian faces I
have seen, or a cat which is about to snarl.
There is intense concentration too. I recognize
one of my father's expressions – a peculiar
way he had of pursing his lips when he had to
make a tremendous effort.

Today my face has changed again. The look of
nervous concentration has slightly softened. I smile
more and look less anxious. The look of resignation I
sometimes wore has gone too. I like my face more. I am
more accepting of it. If it bears the imprint of all my
suffering and experiences of the past few years, then so
be it.

So what have I learned from my experiences over the
last four years that I can pass on to others? First and
foremost, that there is no 'right' way to mourn:
nothing happens in the sequence you expect. You can

and will experience bursts of anger, grief, guilt, regret, pining, even joy at any time. But although you may feel that you are always in danger of regressing, of going back to square one, you do in fact gradually inch forward every time you accomplish even the simplest task which involves contact with another human being or solving a problem. That is why it is so instructive to keep a journal and refer back 'to the way you were'. As in labour, you might think you remember the details of your emotions and actions but in fact you will be quite surprised to rediscover exactly what your pain felt like. This will help you appreciate too how far forward you have moved.

I have learned not to be so hard on myself: to give in to my body when it tells me I should stay in bed an extra couple of hours or that it needs to be cared for in some special way. Be kind to yourself: think of yourself, at least for a while, as ill. You have in all events suffered considerable damage to your sense of self and self-esteem. A death always leaves a person feeling diminished and with the feeling that their universe has shrunk.

It would be the easiest thing in the world to accept a diminished life, but if you do, you are going the way of the dead instead of investing your energies in life. This is why you should welcome the daily struggle that widowhood brings.

Many widows complain that life as a woman alone becomes a battle from morning to night. To them I say, relish the struggle – do battle. It will make you start to feel alive again, even if it involves wearying confrontations with everyone from builders to bank managers. Widowhood is probably the best course in self-assertiveness that could possibly be devised. If you refuse to allow your life to contract, you will feel proud, as I do, of your new ferocity.

You will find too that you do not have to become what others would like to see you become. If you want to stay in the family house, as I did, and there are no financial reasons preventing it, then stay in it, redecorate, revamp, and make it yours.

If you want to travel do. Many single people dread doing this, not only because of shockingly high single room supplements but because they fear the loneliness of being on unfamiliar territory, or in having perhaps to confront themselves for the first time without the usual supports. You may find, as I did, that you have to travel in a different way, that the usual two-week holiday can seem unendurably long for a person on her own, and that short breaks to cities are far more interesting than a beach holiday where you will be nostalgically looking at all the families and couples. In cities you will be likely to meet other people travelling alone – people you can share a meal with or even an excursion. Many single people dread eating alone but I found one way of getting round it was to eat the main meal at midday and just a snack in a café at night. This way you can avoid feeling lonely and conspicuous, and people are much more apt to talk to you during the day.

Every widow discovers that she cannot take her social life for granted any more. I now know that I cannot afford to leave anything to chance. It is especially important to have a 'focus' for the weekend or Bank Holidays. This does not have to be anything more elaborate than a trip to a garden centre, or having a friend to tea. In my case, as an avid theatre goer, I try and take in a matinee at least once a fortnight. I have learned to plan in advance (something I rarely did when I was married) so that I am not left desperately phoning around at the last minute wondering why everybody else has arrangements.

If you work, you probably find the weekdays well taken care of. If you don't, it is important to get some structure into your days, so they don't all tend to merge into each other. Not everyone is cut out for charity work or evening classes; but most people like chatting to others, and the feeling that there is some sense of purpose in their life. Visiting an elderly or sick relative or friend can give you that sense of purpose. Making themselves available to others is a role many widows happily play – but remember to make yourself available to *you* too. Give yourself at least one major treat a week (only you will know what constitutes a treat) whether it is eating out, making an overseas call, or buying yourself something silly to wear – it really doesn't matter. The fact is, it shows that you think you are worth it.

I cannot in all honesty say that I am never lonely, but I have learned that being alone is not the same thing as feeling lonely. I also cannot deny that I do suffer from occasional depression – but then I remind myself that I have good reason to. I don't fight it; on the contrary I allow myself to wallow in it for a while, reassuring myself that it will pass, and it does.

I have learned to cherish my support network: a good neighbour, an accommodating help who will feed the cat while I am away, and a couple of male friends who will heave furniture and lug things from the garden centre. There are also a couple of girlfriends I know I can phone at any time. In the early days they were my lifeline, phoning me once or twice a day from anywhere around the world: it is with them I can share my most vulnerable feelings.

That is another important lesson I have learned: there is no shame in admitting my vulnerability. On the other hand I have learned not to expect support from everyone – that includes even close family and friends. But I also know that their inability to offer support, their lack of empathy, even their avoidance is *their* problem not mine. I have learned to accept and be grateful for help from wherever I can find it. By far the biggest change I had to make was dropping my 'superwoman' act and admitting on occasion that even I could feel helpless, terrified, tired and fallible.

In many ways it is a relief not to have to entertain formally, keep up a round of dinner parties and socializing as well as an immaculate household appearance. On many days I don't even make the bed. On others I polish and scour and fill the house with flowers. The point is I don't have to keep up any standard except my own.

In spite of my feeling that everyone has the ability to cope, I have learned that there is no shame in seeking professional help or therapy. I owe much to my bereavement counsellor and hypnotherapist who worked wonders with visualization exercises that I use to this day to restore a sense of calm when I need to. Many bereaved people avoid seeking help; they feel they don't need it; often they feel they ought to be able to cope on their own and then find later on that all kinds of symptoms such as insomnia, backache, or agoraphobia appear which betray a delayed mourning they have to come to terms with. It is never too late to seek counselling or therapy, even many years after the loss. The important thing is the awareness that you need help and want to change.

While in many cases the widow finds herself stretched to capacity by taking on new roles once performed by her husband – principal wage-earner, family planner and administrator – it is undeniable that in the eyes of society she loses status. Very often the death is followed by the disintegration of a family as a close-knit unit. Often, as in my own case, the children leave home. One of the most difficult aspects of widowhood for me was the onus and responsibility I felt making all the major family decisions alone. Undoubtedly this can make for stress. A 'neutral' friend who knows your family history and the personalities involved can be helpful here, though it is no substitute for making joint decisions with a husband.

I am finding too that the strain of feeling responsible for my children has lessened since I have let go a little and learned to grow with them. The fact that I am groping around like an adolescent myself much of the time in the establishment of my new identity brings me closer to them. The generation gap has been strangely closed in that sense: if both you and your daughter are dating at the same time you can't possibly patronize her in the same way you might be tempted to do as a wife and mother.

Handling all these problems single-handed can not only bring you some measure of satisfaction but it can also make you feel closer to your husband. Many widows feel that their husband is 'guiding' them. I have had this feeling many times in the last few years. I got into the habit of going to the cemetery and asking for Jacques' guidance every time I encountered a problem with the children. Apart from anything else, it seemed to clear my head and restore confidence and eventually a solution always seemed to emerge. Now I no longer feel obliged to find solutions to everything. Perhaps that is the biggest advance of all.

Freud put forward the idea that withdrawal of the libido that attaches one person to another can take place only when the lost person is reinstated within the ego. Many regard identification with the lost object as a necessary component of mourning. I know that the identification I have developed with Jacques in the last few years has enormously helped restore my sense of identity.

Best of all, perhaps, bereavement does not rob you permanently of one of the most precious human faculties – a sense of humour. It never ceases to amaze me that even in your blackest moments, you can laugh – indeed *have* to laugh. On a trip to Hong Kong, I rediscovered a long lost talent for mimicry that I had not used virtually since my teen years, and found I could amuse our group of travel journalists with my imitations of pompous hotel managers and PR representatives. I love to impersonate, and there is nothing more pleasing than to discover that one has even the smallest talent to amuse; this is the gift I think I envy above all else in others. I am very partial to the kind of practical jokes twelve-year-olds enjoy. I have rediscovered not only the 'girl' but the 'child'.

I am conscious of a change in my attitude towards ageing. I find myself getting extremely angry with those who live in dread of growing older, who complain endlessly about the loss of faculties, looks, vitality and opportunities. I am simply grateful now for every extra year – especially when I remember how desperately Jacques (and so many others like him)

wanted just to live to see the next spring. To gather
years, to grow old, is an achievement, a privilege. I will
never again worry about a few grey hairs or lines on
my face.

Every time I walk along the High Street the thought
occurs to me that at least half the people around me
have lost someone close to them; and yet here they are
going about their everyday life coping silently with
the pain. Bereavement is invisible – something we all
know about but usually, except at funerals and
immediately afterwards, choose to ignore unless
confronted head on with it. Bereavement supersedes
all divisions – all classes; in one way it unites us all,
making unwitting survivors of us all. There will be a
period in all our lives when it will seem like an entire
wall of our house has been torn down and we are living
with a cold wind tearing into our guts. One might
imagine that with this knowledge, we would all go
mad. But just as we are the only creatures aware
almost from birth of our own death, so too we are also
fully equipped to survive this knowledge. That much I
know: not only that I can handle the worst of what life
has to offer, and survive. I have learned that I can live
to be happy again – that, if we work through that cold,
bleak winter, then the 'invincible summer' in us all
does finally win through.

Suggested Further Reading

Books

Hill, Susan, *In the Springtime of the Year*, Hamish Hamilton, 1974

Jeffers, Susan, *Feel the Fear and Do It Anyway*, Arrow, 1991

Kübler-Ross, Elisabeth, *On Death and Dying*, Routledge, 1990

Kushner, Harold, *When Bad Things Happen to Good People*, Pan, 1982

Lake, Dr Tony, *Living With Grief*, Sheldon Press, 1984

Lewis, C S, *A Grief Observed*, Faber & Faber, 1961

Parkes, Colin Murray, *Bereavement: Stories of Grief in Adult Life*, Zr.e. Penguin, 1991

Pincus, Lily, *Death in the Family*, Faber & Faber, 1976

Taylor, Liz McNeill, *Living with Loss*, Fontana, 1983

Wylie, Betty Jane, *Beginnings: A Book for Widows*, Unwin, 1986

Useful booklets for the bereaved

Good Grief: Rituals for Dealing With Grief, Elaine Childs Gavell, (Gavell Publications PO Box 58146, Seattle, Washington 98188, USA)

Especially good for providing a practical guide to ways of dealing with grief issues. Creates simple and effective 'grief rituals' that anyone who has ever suffered a loss can use.

Bereavement: What to Expect and How to be Helpful, available from MIND, 22 Harley Street, London W1N 2ED.

What to do After Death, is a helpful booklet available free of charge from the Registrar's office (where all deaths have to be registered) or from your local social security office. This booklet explains what needs to be done, lists organizations and sources of advice, and outlines what social security benefits are available.